Our Brave Foremothers

Celebrating 100 Black, Brown, Asian & Indigenous Women Who Changed the Course of History

ROZELLA KENNEDY
creator of the Brave Sis Project

Illustrated by JOELLE AVELINO

Workman Publishing • New York

In gratitude to our foremothers and all of us Brave Sisses— past, present, and future.

Library of Congress Cataloging-in-Publication Data is available.
ISBN 978-1-5235-1455-7

Design by Becky Terhune

Workman books are available at special discounts when purchased in bulk for premiums and sales promotions as well as for fundraising or educational use. Special editions or book excerpts can also be created to specification. For details, please contact specialmarkets@hbgusa.com.

Workman Publishing Co., Inc., a subsidiary of Hachette Book Group, Inc.
1290 Avenue of the Americas
New York, NY 10104
workman.com

WORKMAN is a registered trademark of Workman Publishing Co., Inc., a subsidiary of Hachette Book Group, Inc.

Printed in China on responsibly sourced paper.
First printing March 2023

10 9 8 7 6 5 4 3 2 1

CONTENTS

INTRODUCTION

When we think about women's history,
who do we consider, and who do we omit?

I was intimidated, as a little girl, when it was time to visit my older aunties. Their dimly lit living rooms, thick upholstered couches covered with yellowing plastic that stuck to the backs of my legs, faded photographic triptychs of Jesus, Martin, and JFK above the kitchen entryway—it was a constrained contrast to the colorful, cacophonous 1970s world outside their windows. Though no longer recent urban transplants, they retained many Down South mannerisms and admonitions: *Don't interrupt (in fact, speak only when asked a question); sit up straight, young lady; go get your mama a cool drink—but don't leave that Frigidaire open too long and run up my light bill. . . .* My younger self, a tomboy who would've rather been playing Wiffle ball with the boys on the neighborhood asphalt diamond, who squawked and guffawed over preteen stuff with my schoolmates, was forced into a rigid mold of respectful ladylikeness.

Little did I realize that these snippets of time and talk—tales of bills, bad boyfriends and churchgoing husbands, Jesus, wayward adult children getting into all kinds of trouble (not the John-Lewis-good-trouble kind of trouble, just baaaad trouble), Jesus, tsk-tsking about the war, fretting about the cost of chicken thighs, the latest thing the mayor wanted to do, the health or illness of relatives Down South, Jesus, and a whole lot of topics that went way over my head—were acts of women inserting themselves into history. Perhaps little *h* history, but as significant as any building block of a person's legacy. By just being alive and somehow managing to keep it together well enough to raise me, my older cousins, and the little ones coming up, by staying safe and sanctified and as whole as they could, these women embodied spirit, resilience, and bravery. Only decades later did I see that these women, my *foremothers*, forged a direct bridge to those who had come before.

It was this very foremother spirit that visited me on Christmas Day in 2019, waking me from sleep with a whisper to "tell my story." When that ancestral voice spoke to me—across centuries, I believe—I felt called to meet as many of these women in history as I could and to make them the center of a creative endeavor, which I called the Brave Sis Project. This soon expanded into a dignified pantheon of women—Black, Brown, Asian, Indigenous—all of whom had far too often been forgotten, ignored, or erased and, in many cases, were as anonymous as my aunties. In your hands, you hold only a petal of this ever-expanding, intergenerational, intercultural bouquet of women being lifted into the significance they deserve.

Our Brave Foremothers presents one hundred women who changed the course of United States history. Some of their names will be familiar, but many might be new to you. Following each profile is a prompt encouraging you to relate the story of every foremother to your own. It is my hope that, in reading about these women, reflecting on their influence, and embracing the prompts, you will kindle some of your own fire, power, and promise. I hope you become inspired to learn more: about them, about yourself, and about other women who have great stories to tell, even if they don't necessarily look like you. This is the book's offering: to help us impact the world in positive ways, as our foremothers did before us.

Delving into history from the stance of a charmed story collector and not an academic has been both a privilege and a challenge. These women live in my heart, and I can't feel so bad about my daily blues when I consider the devotedness of Clara Brown, the fearlessness of Jovita Idár, the guts of Grace Lee Boggs, or the selflessness of Martha Louise Morrow Foxx.

But navigating the constantly evolving linguistic conventions is an unavoidable challenge, since most (but not all) of these foremothers lived during the eighteenth and nineteenth centuries and up to the mid-twentieth century. As viable as they may have been for the time periods, denominations such as "Negro," "Oriental," "homosexual," and "Caucasian" are so jarring that I use them only when absolutely necessary for historical accuracy. At the same time, it felt inauthentic to insert some of today's more inclusive descriptors and concepts into the chronicles of women who lived during a time when sex was conflated with gender; words such as "slave," "slave owner," and "prostitution" were used; there was little awareness about deadnaming; and LGBTQIA+ identities were considered a choice. I've tried to address these facts with sensitivity while maintaining historic fidelity, especially if the speech of the day was important to the story.

Regarding terms related to race or ethnicity, my timeline aligns with the "Power" movements of my childhood: Black people before the 1970s are generally referred to as African American (though at the time, many would've been called Afro-American). Absolute consistency is not the objective, however; sometimes I use the terms interchangeably in the same profile. This is a matter of style more than historic veracity. I've tried to let the geographic, linguistic, and chronological context of each woman guide my use of terms such as Native American vs. American Indian, or Latina vs. Hispanic—but I acknowledge that identity descriptors are often complex and personal.

Sadly, it's also important to note that factual evidence and records pertaining to women, and women of color in particular, have often been obscured and disputed due to the vagaries and lapses in record-keeping— or deliberately erased. You'll see that enslaved people did not regularly have last names because they were considered property, and dates of birth were entered haphazardly for many Black and Native American women because record-keeping was inconsistent—and sometimes intentionally negligent in the case of shackled, displaced, detained, or disregarded people.

So this is not meant to be a history book, but our storybook, something that is alive and in which you can also discover some of your being and life story. You may wish to read linearly from cover to cover, or you just as readily might flip the pages to find a story, illustration, or prompt that speaks to your interests and needs in a given moment. I recommend finding a beautiful notebook or journal for capturing your written reflections, visual creations, and inspirations that arise when reading the book and its prompts.

If learning about these women inspires you to investigate other stories, other erased or forgotten or underappreciated lives, particularly in your own family or community, all the better! It is my dream that together— each in our own space, and perhaps in some collective ways as well—we will write new histories, celebrate more deeply, love more authentically, explore more fully, and be as brave as we each can be—and then beyond that.

Ada Blackjack

1898–MAY 29, 1983

....

Ada Blackjack didn't set out to be a castaway and a survivor. This simple-living Iñupiat woman merely hoped to earn enough money to retrieve her son from the Nome, Alaska, orphanage where she'd placed him after a divorce left her penniless.

Located above the Arctic Circle in Siberia, Wrangel Island is the last place on earth where woolly mammoths lived some four thousand years ago. In the early 1900s, it became the subject of international geopolitical conquest. Though she had no wilderness experience, Ada accepted the job of cook and seamstress on what became a disastrous colonizing expedition. She and four men set off for the large and barren island in September 1921.

Once they reached their destination, they discovered bleak and inhospitable land. As their sojourn carried forth, the explorers found themselves with dwindling rations, scarce game for hunting, and without hope that any rescue ship could penetrate the thick winter ice.

The long and frigid arctic winters brought the party to the brink of starvation, and by the beginning of 1923, they were desperate. Three of the men set off for help one morning, never to be seen again. Ada was left with the one other crew member: scurvy-sick adventurer Lorne Knight. Though Ada learned to hunt and trap and administered medical care, Knight was verbally abusive. When he finally died, Ada didn't have enough strength to bury him, so she simply barricaded his tent against wild animals. Then it was just her and the cat, Vic.

Under such duress, Ada's will to survive kicked in—perhaps the Iñupiat ways of knowing and living imparted to her by her forebears were awakened within her. Her hunting skills improved; she erected a lookout platform from driftwood so she could watch for polar bears; and she even used animal carcasses to rebuild the

---

"I thank God for living." —A.B.

---

boat. When Ada was finally rescued in August 1923, the crew members said she could have survived another year—not that anyone wished that!

After the celebration died down, Ada was accused of exaggerating her story, and the speculator who commissioned the expedition became famous for his account of the ordeal, even though he hadn't been there. Ada Blackjack's own diary fell into obscurity for many years, and she remained destitute for much of her life.

Try logging off your devices for two or three days to see what you can learn about yourself when you're not doomscrolling, watching TV, or burying yourself in your feed. (You can do it!)

Mary Ellen Pleasant

AUGUST 19, 1814–JANUARY 4, 1904

When Mary Ellen Pleasant was six years old, her mother disappeared, and she was sent to work as a domestic servant for a white abolitionist family in the free state of Massachusetts. Light-skinned, she was able to pass for white, as was her first husband, a merchant named James Smith. Thus privileged, they amassed a sizable fortune, which she inherited when he died four years into their marriage.

In 1848, she remarried, to John "J. J." Pleasant. Fearing for her safety due to her antislavery activism, she fled Massachusetts, first to New Orleans (where she may have apprenticed to "Voodoo Queen" Marie Laveau—see page 60) and eventually to San Francisco in 1852, to join her husband and the Gold Rush boom. The couple worked to extend the Underground Railroad coast to coast in defiance of the state governor's wishes to rewrite California law and permit the capture and re-enslavement of free Black people. Using her inheritance, Mary Ellen provided money, food, and shelter to help people escape this fate. She also gave financial support to John Brown's foiled 1859 Harper's Ferry Raid. Indeed, when Brown was hanged for his conspiracy, the executioners found a note in his pocket that had Mary Ellen's first initial flipped: WEP instead of MEP. Whether a misspelling or deliberate, it likely saved her life as it disguised her identity and connection to Brown.

She also fought against discrimination, suing the San Francisco trolley companies several times in the 1860s and '70s over their refusal to pick up Black passengers. She even staged a streetcar sit-in in 1866. Her reputation earned her two nicknames: the Mother of Civil Rights

> "I often wonder what I would have been with an education. I have let books alone and studied men and women a good deal." —M.E.P.

in California and the Harriet Tubman of California.

Meanwhile, Mary Ellen continued to grow her fortune in San Francisco, opening a restaurant and several laundries and boardinghouses. Disguising herself as the cook or a domestic, she gained access to wealthy white Gold Rush merchants, who tipped her off to investment opportunities in gold and silver. Knowing that a woman would be scrutinized for such financial savvy, Mary Ellen placed her business dealings in the name of Thomas Bell, a boarder in her rooming house. The business partners amassed a combined fortune that neared $900 million in today's dollars.

Mary Ellen, Thomas, and the wife she found for him lived together in a San Francisco mansion that was the subject of much speculation. Some said it was a brothel; others said Mary Ellen practiced frightful voodoo rituals in the basement. Most enduring of the rumors was that Mary Ellen and Thomas were lovers— gossip that was perhaps bolstered by the fact that J. J. Pleasant had disappeared from the public record, whereabouts unknown. Despite the hubbub, Mary Ellen Pleasant rose up San Francisco's social register— until the Civil War ended, and she revealed herself to the community as a Black woman. Rejected and mocked (the newspapers referred to her as "Mammy Pleasant," a name that stuck), she was also sued by Thomas's widow after his death and left penniless.

Mary Ellen wanted her tombstone to read "Friend of John Brown," yet her wish was not granted until 1965. What are five things you would like people in future centuries to know about you?

Rose Fortune

MARCH 13, 1774–FEBRUARY 20, 1864

The formidable Rose Fortune was born to Black Loyalists of African and South American descent who sided with the British during the Revolutionary War in exchange for the promise of emancipation. After the war ended, Rose's family was among the approximately three thousand Black Loyalists who were relocated to the British territory of Nova Scotia in present-day Canada. Rose's childhood is not well documented, but it's known that as an adult she had a business at the Annapolis Royal Wharf where she used a wheelbarrow to transport the baggage of new arrivals to nearby homes and hotels.

Rose became known on the waterfront as an honest, hardworking, and reliable businesswoman. Over time, she expanded her services, replacing the wheelbarrow with a horse-drawn wagon and escorting people to the docks for maritime departures. Rose was so good at

> "You come right along, jedge. No time to be sleeping now. Yo'all got to hold co'at in Digby, and yo'know right well you got to ketch that boat." —R.F.

keeping an eye on the waterfront that the community essentially considered her the police officer of Annapolis Royal, making her one of the first known women policing public safety in North America. No youthful horseplay, no drunken rabble-rousing, no foolishness allowed! She also helped runaway slaves reach freedom in Canada through the Underground Railroad.

To this day, there seems to be only one image of Rose: a watercolor sketch of a woman in profile holding a small basket and wearing a straw hat, a thick dress, a kerchief, and a heavy overcoat. She is caught midstride, looking purposeful. A memorial plaque at the Annapolis Royal Wharf reads, "The story of Rose Fortune epitomizes the perseverance of Black Loyalists who confronted prejudice and inequality to make a place for themselves in Canada."

Her descendants remained in the stevedore and transportation business until well into the twentieth century. One of them, Daurene Lewis, became the first Black woman mayor in Canada when she was elected in Annapolis Royal in 1984.

If you were appointed head of your local peacekeeping force, how would you try to keep people abiding by the law? What would be the most important rules, and how would you enforce them?

ANNAPOLIS ROYAL
WHARF

Pura Belpré

BETWEEN 1899 AND 1903–JULY 1, 1982

While New York City in the 1920s was the center of the Harlem Renaissance, it also became home to the first of several waves of Puerto Rican immigrants. The Jones-Shafroth Act granted US citizenship to Puerto Ricans in 1917, but cultural separation was common. Though some people at the time considered libraries to be spaces that upheld the glory of the English language and Anglo-Saxon culture, Pura Belpré had different ideas.

Hired as the city's first Latina librarian in 1921, Pura became a chronicler and champion of Puerto Rican folklore and the wonder of childhood. At the New York Public Library branch on 115th Street in East Harlem, she put on regular events, such as puppet shows and bilingual story hours, and introduced new traditions, such as the celebration of Día de Reyes. These efforts helped define the East Harlem branch as a cultural magnet of Latino New York.

She also wrote books; 1932's *Perez y Martina* is a charming tale of love between a cockroach and a mouse, and it was the first children's book published in Spanish by a mainstream press in the United States. As her career grew, she translated the folktales of her homeland into English, helping a new generation of Boricua

> "To appreciate the present, one must have a knowledge of the past. . . . To know where we go, we must know from where we came." —P.B.

New Yorkers learn that reading, literature, and storytelling belonged to them as well.

By the 1960s, libraries were not just places to read and borrow books but essential neighborhood centers, providing a range of social services to community members. Pura helped lead the newly established South Bronx Library Project, which integrated wraparound social services with library resources. For her many contributions, she received the

NYC Mayor's Award for Arts and Culture in 1982, just months before her passing.

Today, the annual Pura Belpré Award, which was founded in 1996, is presented by the American Library Association to a Latinx writer and illustrator "whose work best portrays, affirms, and celebrates the Latino cultural experience in an outstanding work of literature for children and youth." The legacy of this inspiring cultural champion lives on.

Stop by your local library or community center to speak with a librarian, thank them for all they do, and check out what types of community events are hosted there.

Fannie Lou Hamer

OCTOBER 6, 1917–MARCH 14, 1977

F annie Lou Hamer was born into a world of broken promises. The Fifteenth Amendment, passed in 1870, forty-seven years before her birth, promised suffrage for African American men—not women. The Nineteenth Amendment, passed when she was three, gave women the right to vote—but Black women's voting rights were still limited. Further, Jim Crow laws, discriminatory voting practices, lynching, and more kept the formerly enslaved disenfranchised, ostracized, and terrorized. It was time for a justice revolution, and Fannie, the twentieth and last-born child of Mississippi sharecroppers, was destined to make her mark.

Though academically promising, she could attend a one-room schoolhouse in rural Mississippi only in the summer, when cotton was fallow. One of her legs was damaged by a childhood bout with polio, and she was later subjected to involuntary sterilization, or, as the procedures were ruefully called, "Mississippi appendectomies."

> "We been waitin' all our lives and still gettin' killed, still gettin' hung, still gettin' beat to death. Now we're tired waitin'!" —F.L.H.

In 1962, Fannie became active with the Southern Christian Leadership Conference, gathering signatures for a petition to provide federal aid for African American families in need. She also worked with the Student Nonviolent Coordinating Committee on voter reform. Fannie eventually rose to the role of field secretary and finally voted for the first time in 1963.

Fannie's heroism came at enormous cost. She was intimidated, detained, and even shot at. One of her adopted daughters hemorrhaged to death because the local hospital refused to admit her, as a way of punishing Fannie for her political agitation. An atrociously brutal police

beating in 1963 left her nearly dead and with permanent kidney damage. Three days after this assault, the state field director of the National Association for the Advancement of Colored People (NAACP), Medgar Evers, was assassinated.

Even in the face of such clear and present danger, Fannie's faith and her tenacious dedication to the rights of women, children, and Black people never wavered. She became an increasingly central figure in Martin Luther King Jr.'s Poor People's Campaign, helped organize the Freedom Summer voting drive in 1964, and cofounded the Mississippi Freedom Democratic Party, which protested the state's all-white delegation to the 1964 Democratic National Convention. She even ran for the Mississippi Senate in 1971.

Education and economic justice were also important causes to Fannie Lou Hamer. She cofounded the National Women's Political Caucus with Shirley Chisholm (see page 20) and Florynce "Flo" Kennedy (see page 72); helped establish the federal Head Start program for early childhood education; and in 1968, formed the Freedom Farm Cooperative, where former sharecroppers could buy and farm their land collectively.

Spirituals and other traditional songs gave Fannie and her peers courage in trying times. What song or poem inspires you most? Share it with people you know and see how it resonates.

Kateri Tekakwitha

1656–APRIL 17, 1680

When European settlers arrived in the Americas, they brought with them infectious pathogens, such as the rabidly contagious and highly fatal smallpox, to which Indigenous populations had no immunity. Some scholars estimate that these diseases decimated up to 90 percent of some Native communities in South, Central, and North America. Several historians and epidemiologists posit that the diseases were willfully introduced to subjugate Indigenous peoples.

The young Algonquin and Mohawk girl who would later be known as Kateri was only four years old when her parents and brother succumbed to smallpox in 1660. Though she survived, the virus damaged her eyesight and left her face badly scarred. She was teased for her impairments and called Tekakwitha, which means "she who bumps into things."

Kateri was adopted by an uncle, and at age eight, she was groomed for marriage, per Algonquin and Mohawk tradition. Moved by the message of Christian missionaries, she defied the path set out for her and officially converted to Catholicism at age nineteen, against the wishes of her family. Facing hostility and threats to her life, she escaped persecution by traveling to the Mission of St. Francis Xavier, a Native American Catholic community near Montreal, Canada.

Consecrating herself to the Virgin Mary, Kateri received the sacrament of Holy Communion in 1679. In her new vocation, she instructed children in the catechism and attended to sick and older

"The poverty I am threatened with does not scare me, because so little is needed to give to the necessities of this miserable life and my labor could provide for it and I could always find some rags to cover me." —K.T.

people. To prove her devotion, she practiced mortification of the flesh: fasting, sleeping on beds of thorns, and other repentances that Catholics associated with the expiation of sin. The combination of illness and deprivation may have been what led her to an early grave soon after her twenty-fourth birthday. The Jesuit priests who attended to her last rites attested that not an hour after her death, the pockmarks on her face miraculously disappeared, leaving her visage radiant.

In her biography, Father Pierre Cholenec's *Catherine Tekakwitha: Her Life*, it's said that Kateri appeared in prophetic visions to people in prayer in 1680 and in the subsequent two years. These sightings and other miracles, seen as the fulfillment of her deathbed promise to pray for her loved ones in heaven, form the core of her long-standing cult of dedication throughout the Americas. Canonized by Pope Benedict XVI in 2012, she is considered an honorary patroness of Montreal, Canada; of Catholic Native Americans in the United States; and in Mexico, where the first convent for Native American nuns was established fifty years after her death. Known as the "Lily of the Mohawks," Kateri Tekakwitha is now celebrated as the patroness of ecology and the environment.

If you were a saint (of any or no religion), what would you be the patron of? What kinds of images or shapes would be in your stained-glass window?

Angela Davis

JANUARY 26, 1944–

The 1960s were a time of enormous change in the United States, with Vietnam War protests, second-wave feminism, the civil rights movement, and other progressive causes rising and colliding during social and political upheaval. The unapologetically radical professor, philosopher, and author Angela Davis rejected the bourgeois aspirations of many midcentury Black Americans; the legacies of slavery, racism, and capitalism were too great to ignore. Today, she is one of the country's most respected political voices, but once upon a time, she was, to the FBI, Public Enemy Number One.

Born in Mississippi at the height of the Jim Crow era, Angela grew up experiencing racism and oppression. As a young adult and scholar, she was influenced by philosopher and political theorist Herbert Marcuse, who believed the affluent modern society represses everyone, even the wealthy. The young Professor Davis experienced a roller coaster of hirings and firings due to her membership in the Che-Lumumba Club (an all-Black branch of the Communist Party) and the Black Panthers and her role as a protest leader.

Black liberation radicalism exploded in 1970 with the plot to free imprisoned Black activist George Jackson. The guns used in the failed hostage-taking ploy belonged to Angela, and after a two-month hunt she was captured and jailed for eighteen months in what was potentially a capital case. In Nixon's America, the Free Angela movement became one of the most popular social causes for those who supported her antiracist, antiwar, anticapitalist, and antisexist agenda. When she was acquitted in 1972, Angela returned to lecturing, providing commentary on social and cultural academic issues, and organizing to dismantle the system of incarceration.

Today, Angela is a highly respected scholar whose work reaches both academe and the streets. She has authored more than ten books about history, incarceration, abolition, women, and culture. In 1997, she came out as a lesbian and added LGBTQIA+ issues to the broad list of topics on which she speaks and writes regularly. Despite, or perhaps because of, her "notorious" past, Angela Davis remains a trusted voice for generations of womanists and activists worldwide.

"After decades of being the backbone of civil rights movements, women have finally come to the forefront in the US." —A.D.

Think of someone, either from history or the present day, whose incarceration would inspire you to campaign for their release. Who would it be, and why?

Chien-Shiung Wu

MAY 31, 1912–FEBRUARY 16, 1997

I n 1957, Chinese American nuclear physicist Chien-Shiung Wu proved that the concept of parity—that every physical process has an identical opposite process—was false, changing how scientists viewed the structure of the universe. Ironically, history also reveals an imbalance in gender: Chien-Shiung's men colleagues were awarded the Nobel Prize in physics that year, but Chien-Shiung—the scientist who actually proved the theories—was overlooked.

Such gender discrimination would have been unwelcome for any woman, but for Chien-Shiung, who grew up in an egalitarian family, it was a distinct departure from the mores of her childhood in early twentieth-century China. While it was uncommon for girls to attend school, Chien-Shiung was able to obtain an education at the school founded by her father. She learned at a young age that girls and women could achieve on a level with boys and men. After earning a master's degree from Nanjing University (as it's known today), Chien-Shiung arrived in the US in 1936 to pursue a PhD in physics at the University of California, Berkeley. By 1942, after a stint teaching at Smith College, she had married and moved to the East Coast, where she was the first

> "In China there are many, many women in physics. There is a misconception in America that women scientists are all dowdy spinsters. This is the fault of men." —C.S.W.

woman professor hired to Princeton University's physics department. In 1944, she began working on Columbia University's Manhattan Project, reportedly becoming the only Chinese person and one of the few women participating in the research that developed the atomic bomb.

In addition to the anti-Asian xenophobia of the midcentury, sexism hounded Chien-Shiung throughout

contributions to the field of physics. In 1958, she was the first woman to be awarded an honorary doctorate of science by Princeton University, and the seventh woman elected to the National Academy of Sciences. In 1975, she became the first woman president of the American Physical Society and also achieved an important milestone: earning pay equal to that of the men professors. Three years later, she became the first person to receive the Wolf Prize in physics; the international award often presages the winner of the Nobel Prize.

her career, particularly as a woman pioneer in a man-dominated field. Like the Nobel snub, she was often passed over for more prestigious assignments. But she continued her work, receiving distinguished awards for her many discoveries and

Chien-Shiung Wu was also the first scientist to have an asteroid named after her during her lifetime: She is honored by 2752 Wu Chien-Shiung, an Eoan asteroid from the outer regions of the asteroid belt discovered in 1965 by astronomers in her college town, Nanjing.

In 2021, Chien-Shiung was posthumously honored with her portrait on a USPS Forever Stamp. Who would you like to see on a postage stamp? Come up with three designs.

Shirley Chisholm

NOVEMBER 30, 1924–JANUARY 1, 2005

....

Shirley Chisholm didn't want to be remembered for her remarkable "firsts": first Black woman elected to the US Congress; first African American to run for president with a major party; and cofounder of both the Congressional Black Caucus and, with Fannie Lou Hamer (see page 12) and Florynce "Flo" Kennedy (see page 72), the National Women's Political Caucus. Instead, she said, "I'd like them to say that Shirley Chisholm had guts. That's how I'd like to be remembered."

Gutsy she was. As young girls, Shirley and her sisters were sent by their Bajan mother and Guyanese father—both working-class émigrés and followers of Marcus Garvey's Pan-Africanist movement—to Barbados to live with their grandmother. Their grandmother's influence and their time spent at a formal British colonial school shaped the girls' self-confidence and rigor. After returning to Brooklyn and earning her master's in education, Shirley got a job as a primary school educator.

In 1953, she became involved in politics by volunteering for local Black candidates and later with the League of Women Voters and the Brooklyn Democratic Club, whose Black membership she helped expand. In 1965, against the backdrop of the civil rights and feminist movements, Shirley was elected to the New York State Assembly, where she fought for domestic workers' pay rights, college access for disadvantaged youth, and expanded food stamp benefits, among other causes. Seeking to further her progressive political agenda, in 1968 Shirley became the first Black woman elected to Congress, representing New York's twelfth congressional district. She staffed her office entirely with women.

When she announced her presidential candidacy in late 1971, many dismissed her campaign as an extraordinarily gutsy but underfunded and largely symbolic act. Shirley felt that sexism was even more detrimental to her political career than racism: "When I ran for the Congress, when I ran for president, I met more discrimination as a woman than for being Black. Men are men," she said.

After retiring from Congress in 1983, Shirley returned to academia and leveraged her platform to cofound the National Congress of Black Women. It would be almost forty years after her retirement that a Black woman would accede to the West Wing, but we all owe gutsy Shirley Chisholm a debt of gratitude.

If you ran for president, what would be the ten most important issues of your platform?

Bharati Mukherjee

JULY 27, 1940–JANUARY 28, 2017

Born to a wealthy family in Kolkata, India, Bharati Mukherjee was educated in London and Basel, Switzerland, as well as in prestigious schools and universities in India. Bharati enrolled in the well-reputed Iowa Writers' Workshop at the University of Iowa, where she earned an MFA and met her husband, with whom she moved to Montreal in 1966. She began her teaching career at McGill University during a time of societal and racial flux. The experience of having been among the social elite in India and Europe and then being seen

as an unwanted immigrant— an "other"—in Canada led her to a deeper exploration of identity and consciousness. Life in Canada proved so frustrating that Bharati and her husband immigrated to the US in 1980.

In America, Bharati went on to become one of the country's most celebrated novelists, short story authors, and professors. In her award-winning works, such as *The Middleman and Other Stories* (1988) and *Jasmine* (1989), Bharati depicted Brown people from across the vast Asian diaspora and elsewhere, all trying to recast their destinies in the

United States. Their struggles and successes reflect a post–1960s and '70s America embracing broader definitions of identity, race, and culture.

Before the second half of the twentieth century, many people of color had an ambiguous relationship with the potentiality of being seen as anything other than white. South Asians in America went through different phases of identification, depending on the vagaries of the law and the census—sometimes categorized as Aryan, Caucasian (literally of the Caucasus region), or white, and other times classified as non-white. For many Brown Americans, the aftermath of British colonialism, colorism in India and elsewhere, and a desire to avoid being grouped with Black Americans at the "bottom" of the social pyramid created a confusing landscape and a complex navigation of melanin and identity that continues today.

> "Most Indian writers prior to this have still thought of themselves as Indians, and their literary inspiration has come from India. India has been the source, and home. Whereas I'm saying, those are wonderful roots, but now my roots are here and my emotions are here in North America." —B.M.

While Bharati Mukherjee herself did ascribe struggles of color and class to the protagonists in her works, her nuanced portraits of the immigrant experience represented the advent of a new generation of activists and artists of color. As one of the first South Asian writers to gain renown in the United States, she recognized her role as a cultural chronicler of a country wrestling with heterogeneity.

How have you seen the immigrant experience in the United States transform the country through food, culture, and other ways? What is most exciting to you?

Bessie Stringfield

1911 OR 1912–FEBRUARY 16, 1993

When you think of a motorcycle rider, who do you see? Chances are it's not a nineteen-year-old, five-foot-two Black woman astride a 1928 Indian Scout bike, riding solo across the United States. And in the 1930s, before both the she-ro archetype of Rosie the Riveter and the interstate highway system, the story of Bessie Stringfield was absolutely remarkable.

Little is known about Bessie's childhood, but she often said she was adopted at age five by an Irish family after her Jamaican father and Dutch mother died of smallpox. While this tale may be apocryphal, it is true that she received her dream gift—a motorcycle—for her sixteenth birthday and taught herself to ride and do stunts.

After high school, Bessie started traveling around the country by herself on her bike, flipping a penny to determine where to go next. In keeping with her free-spirited nature, she earned a living by entering contests (often disguised as a man) and doing stunts like riding on walls or upside down at carnivals and fairs. Another fun fact: "Stringfield" is actually the surname of Bessie's third husband—she had six of them in total, all more than twenty years her junior.

But for a Black woman in the 1930s, all was not fun and games. Bessie had to learn to do her own repairs on rambling, unkempt back roads because mechanics wouldn't help her, and she frequently had to sleep on her bike because of hotel segregation. Yet as the Great Depression wore on, she toured across the US and in Europe, Brazil, and Haiti. She also volunteered as an army courier during World War II—though she was the only woman in her unit—and loved it. Postwar, she settled in Florida, working as a nurse and a domestic. She founded a motorcycle club and continued to amaze people with stunts on her latest bike, a Harley-Davidson.

Bessie rode right up until her death at age eighty-two. Every year, the Bessie Stringfield All-Female Ride welcomes hundreds of women motorcyclists on a cross-country trek.

"All along the way, wherever I rode, the people were overwhelmed to see a Negro woman riding a motorcycle." —B.S.

The Motorcycle Queen of Miami

In 2002, Bessie was posthumously inducted into the Motorcycle Hall of Fame. What special talent or stunt are you (or do you wish to be) known for?

Kalpana Chawla

MARCH 17, 1962–FEBRUARY 1, 2003

There are only two American women of Indian descent with streets named after them in the US; one is Kala Bagai (see page 58), and the other is Kalpana Chawla, who was born in March 1962. Her family altered her birth date to July 1, 1961, so she could take college exams early. Kalpana went on to earn an undergrad degree in India and two master's degrees and a PhD in aerospace engineering in the US before embarking on a career in aeronautical research. She applied to the NASA Astronaut Corps in 1996 and, as a crew member of the space shuttle *Columbia* in 1997, became the first Indian woman and the second South Asian person to go into space. The voyage orbited Earth 252 times, traveling more than 10.4 million miles—a dream come true for the woman who had been obsessed with aircraft since childhood.

> "I never truly thought of being the first or second someone. . . . This is just something I wanted to do. It was very important for me to enjoy it. If you want to do something, what does it matter where you are ranked? Nor does being a woman make a difference. We were all just crew members."
>
> —K.C.

During this mission, the shuttle experienced a technical glitch that could have imperiled the flight. At first, Kalpana was suspected of committing an engineering oversight that precipitated the mishap, but an investigation eventually cleared her of culpability. Eager to return to space, she finally lifted off again on January 16, 2003—*Columbia*'s twenty-eighth mission, STS-107. Tragically, another technical glitch cost the entire crew their lives: Shedding of the spaceship's foam insulation caused the craft to break apart as it reentered

Earth's atmosphere. It was the worst US spacecraft disaster since the 1986 *Challenger* explosion. Kalpana's remains were scattered in Utah's Zion National Park. "She always dreamt of the stars and somehow I feel she dissolved into the stars that day," her father said.

Scientific trailblazer Kalpana Chawla received many posthumous awards, including the Congressional Space Medal of Honor, and she remains a revered role model for girls in STEM and a legend to South Asians all over the world.

Write a letter to a childhood she-ro of yours and tell them how their influence made a difference in your life.

Anna May Wong

JANUARY 3, 1905–FEBRUARY 3, 1961

B orn to second-generation Chinese laundromat owners, Wong Liu
Tsong was often bullied by her racist classmates while attending
elementary school in the Los Angeles area. Movies offered an escape,
literally and figuratively: She'd play hooky and watch film shoots.
Her persistent presence paid off, and she started scoring bit roles
at age fourteen. Three years later, under her new stage name—
Anna May Wong—she was cast as the lead of a tragic love story called
The Toll of the Sea.

Although she eventually became a
style icon (with bangs that were trendy
during the flapper era), Anna May
faced massive discrimination. Anti-
miscegenation laws forbade Asians
from kissing white people onscreen, so
classic Hollywood romance roles were
out of reach. As was the case for most
actresses of color of the era, fetishistic
typecasting dictated the roles that

were available to her: the sexpot (such as her 1924 breakout role in *The Thief of Bagdad*, in which her acting skills were upstaged by her barely-there bandeau top), the dragon lady (1927's *The Devil Dancer*), or the subservient Asian woman. After being passed over for the lead role in 1928's *The Crimson City*, Anna May was cast in a bit role and had to teach Myrna Loy, the white actress playing the Asian lead, how to use chopsticks. Despite poor castings, Anna May was a powerhouse actress able to command deeply moving emotional portrayals, even during the silent film era.

In 1928, Anna May moved to Europe, where she filmed in Berlin, Paris, and London; mastered speaking French and German; and appeared on the West End stage in London. She befriended legendary actress Marlene Dietrich and later starred alongside her in the 1932 film *Shanghai Express*, which many consider to be Anna May's star moment. Still, there was a thirteen-to-one disparity in their pay.

When she returned to Hollywood, Anna May suffered her worst career insult: After her audition for the lead in the 1937 film adaptation of Pearl S. Buck's hit novel, *The Good Earth*, the role went to a white actress who performed in yellow-face. Anna May Wong, the one Asian movie star considered for the film, was offered the only unsympathetic role, which she refused. She retired from movies in 1947, but returned to the screen four years later as a gallery owner and detective in the short-lived TV series *The Gallery of Madame Liu-Tsong*, making history as the first Asian American to headline a television show.

Due to the xenophobic constraints of Anna May's time, interracial kisses were banned in Hollywood movies. This prohibition limited the careers of actresses of color, who could not win "leading lady" roles. When have you subverted a stereotype that someone tried to impose on you because of your identity?

Mary Ann Shadd Cary

OCTOBER 9, 1823–JUNE 5, 1893

The Fugitive Slave Act of 1850 decreed that runaway slaves be returned to their owners, even if they were living in Northern states. Even African Americans who were not born into enslavement, such as Solomon Northup of *Twelve Years a Slave* renown, were subject to capture. Facing such hostile conditions, Mary Ann Shadd Cary and her brother fled Pennsylvania to Ontario, Canada. She encouraged others to join her, writing an 1852 pamphlet that recommended the best places in Canada for American fugitive slaves to settle.

With her education from a Pennsylvania Quaker boarding school, a familial affiliation with the Underground Railroad, and a determined temperament, Mary was unconcerned with the niceties of ladylike behavior. Her first published letter, written in 1848 to abolitionist Frederick Douglass, urged Black leaders to stop merely holding conventions "whining over our difficulties and afflictions [and] passing resolutions on resolutions." Her friends and family nicknamed her "the Rebel."

Mary continued expressing her abolitionist beliefs. In 1853, she founded the antislavery newspaper *Provincial Freeman*, which became an extraordinarily popular showcase for African American expression as well as a forum for intellectual discourse around the news and events of the politically heated antebellum period. In doing so, she became North America's first Black newspaperwoman.

Mary married a man named Thomas Cary and bore two children. To raise money for the newspaper and to help runaway slaves, she became a public speaker, giving lectures throughout the US and

> **"Self-reliance is the fine road to independence."**
>
> —Motto of the *Provincial Freeman*

Ferry Raid—a foiled effort to incite an armed slave revolt in October 1859. Balancing business ownership, however, was too tall a task, and the newspaper, which had always struggled financially despite its social value, ceased publication.

During the Civil War, Mary returned to the US to recruit Northern Black Americans to join the Union Army. Once the war ended, she accepted teaching positions in Wilmington, Delaware, and nearby Washington, DC; she also became an active suffragist, joining the National Woman Suffrage Association. In 1874, Mary Ann Shadd Cary took the dais at the House Judiciary Committee to advocate for the right to vote— decades before the Nineteenth Amendment and generations before the Voting Rights Act.

Canada on social issues such as emancipation and suffrage. Juggling motherhood and activism, she became a friend and financial supporter of abolitionist John Brown, the famous instigator of the Harper's

At age sixty, Mary earned a law degree from Howard University, becoming the second Black woman in the US to earn such a distinction (the first was Charlotte E. Ray; see page 158). Name something you keep planning on doing "later"—how could you make it happen sooner? What steps can you commit to *now*?

Lucy Gonzalez Parsons

1851–MARCH 7, 1942

When a fire erupted at Lucy Gonzalez Parsons's home on March 7, 1942, not only was the ninety-one-year-old labor organizer, radical socialist, and anarcho-communist killed, but many of her writings and historically significant artifacts also went up in flames. It was considered a suspicious inferno; a self-taught and forceful orator and a radical Communist, Lucy was often harassed by the police, even in her elder years. Perhaps she simply embodied too many forms of menace for the authorities to tolerate.

Born into slavery in Virginia, she was relocated in 1863 to Waco, Texas, with her owner (who had impregnated Lucy's mother and was thus also her father). In 1871, Lucy—who had Mexican and Indigenous ancestry in addition to her African American parentage—married white former Confederate soldier and Ku Klux Klan critic Albert Parsons. Though they wed at a time when interracial marriage was legal in Texas, the union caused an uproar and the Parsons left for Chicago.

After settling into a German socialist neighborhood, the couple became active in radical political circles. In 1884, Albert founded an anarchist newspaper called *The Alarm*. As editor and columnist, Lucy denounced the wealthy and encouraged unemployed workers to seek revenge on the affluent—with explosives, if necessary. On May 1, 1886, the couple, along with their two children, helped lead the world's first May Day parade, rallying eighty thousand people around the

> "Strike not for a few cents more an hour, because the price of living will be raised faster still, but strike for all you earn, be content with nothing less." —L.G.P.

United States to demand an eight-hour workday.

Their dream of establishing a cashless, cooperative society came crashing down three days later when a bomb detonated in Chicago's Haymarket Square, killing seven police officers and many civilians.

The authorities needed a way to neutralize radicals, and Albert was seen as a clear and present danger. While his involvement in the bombing was unsubstantiated—some say he and Lucy were having a meal blocks away at the time—he and three other men were hanged.

Lucy redoubled her activism by organizing picket lines, leading working women into wealthy neighborhoods to confront the rich on their doorsteps, and conducting speaking tours throughout the United States and in England. In 1905, she and Mother Jones were the only two women delegates at the founding convention of the Industrial Workers of the World, but Lucy was no longer seen as the vanguard of the movement. Toward the end of her life, Lucy Gonzalez Parsons was destitute, and when the police seized books and personal papers that survived the inferno, much of her legacy was silenced.

While FDR's New Deal era was a watershed period for working people's rights and well-being, Lucy dismissed it as an effort to placate workers and delay the inevitable overthrow of capitalism. Channel her anger and energy into writing a letter to a newspaper editor about a current social issue you find intolerable.

Clara Hale

APRIL 1, 1905–DECEMBER 18, 1992

An orphan at age sixteen, Clara Hale had a great deal of determination. She was the first in her family to graduate high school, and she got married soon thereafter, working as a maid while studying business administration. In the midst of the Great Depression, when so many were struggling, her husband died of cancer, leaving Clara with two biological children and an adopted son. Seeking a means to provide for her children financially as well as care for them physically, she established a childcare service at her home in Harlem. The environment she created for the little ones provided so much stability that before long, many of the local children wanted to live with her full time. By 1940, Clara was serving as a foster parent, too.

At the time, many in the Harlem community were falling victim to the compounded societal ills of the midcentury. By the late 1960s, heroin addiction was a full-on public health crisis in much of New York but proved particularly acute in underserved communities far from the city's centers of wealth and power. When

> "If you can't hold children in your arms, please hold them in your heart." —C.H.

Clara's adult daughter passed a mother nodding off on the street, her newborn nearly falling to the ground, she knew that superhero forces were needed to rehabilitate this family's situation. She went to her sixty-four-year-old mother and begged her to take in the child. This was the genesis of Hale House, an institution that has since served generations of New Yorkers.

Clara responded to the needs of children first: She found permanent homes for kids who were living without homes or in unstable situations. Noticing that so many young parents were struggling with raising children, she also began teaching childcare essentials. By 1969, Hale House, now an official charity, was coordinating with city authorities and local groups to provide young mothers with resources of all sorts. When the AIDS catastrophe hit in the 1980s, Hale House added additional health and social service accommodations.

Over the years, Hale House arranged care for more than a thousand infants and toddlers and countless juveniles and adults, many of whom were cast off by a society that considered them too far gone to help. To New Yorkers and others in national humanitarian circles, the woman known as Mother Hale was an American version of Mother Teresa.

What do you consider to be your "safe place"?
Who or what makes you feel that way?

Mary Golda Ross

AUGUST 9, 1908–APRIL 29, 2008

Mary Golda Ross came from a proud lineage: Her great-great-grandfather, Cherokee chief John Ross, was the longest-serving tribal leader of his people. Valiantly resisting the US seizure of Cherokee lands until the final forced relocation in the 1830s, her family, like many in the tribe, maintained certain traditions, including gender equality in education. For this reason, Mary's parents sent her away from the reservation to live with her grandparents in Tahlequah, Oklahoma, where the schools were better. Mary hardly minded being the only girl in her math class—a precursor to her future as a groundbreaking woman in STEM.

During the Great Depression, Mary worked for the betterment of Indigenous people, first as a science and math teacher in rural Oklahoma, next as a statistician for the Bureau of Indian Affairs, and later as a girls' advisor at the Santa Fe Indian School (now known as the Institute of American Indian Arts) in New Mexico.

In 1941, she moved to California with her master's degree in hand to see how her mathematics training could help the war effort. Lockheed, the pioneering aeronautical corporation, hired her a year later, making her the first American Indian woman engineer in the United States. Equipped with a pencil, a slide rule, and a brilliant mathematical mind, she helped conceptualize the fastest new airplanes and contributed designs for interplanetary spaceflight—an idea that, at the time, resided entirely in the realm of the fantastical.

> **"I was the only female in my class. I sat on one side of the room and the guys on the other side of the room. I guess they didn't want to associate with me. But I could hold my own with them, and sometimes did better."** —M.G.R.

After the war, women who had taken up factory work were expected to relinquish their jobs to men reentering the workforce. But Lockheed sent Mary to UCLA to obtain a professional certification in aeronautics and missile and celestial mechanics. In 1952, she became one of the forty founding engineers of the highly autonomous Skunk Works project. This was an ultrasecretive federal effort that pioneered exploration of Earth-orbiting flights, satellites, missions to Venus and Mars, and other facets of space travel. Much of Mary's research and writing at Lockheed remains classified, even today.

After retirement, she continued to mentor women and Native American youth in the STEM fields. When the National Museum of the American

Indian opened as part of the Smithsonian Institution in 2004, Mary Golda Ross appeared as an honored guest in a traditional Cherokee calico dress.

In a 1958 episode of the popular TV quiz show *What's My Line?*, celebrity contestants had to guess Mary's role as someone who "designs rocket missiles and satellites." Contestants were stumped, as no one expected a woman to hold that role. If you were on the show today, what would your identifying description be?

Felicisima "Ping" Serafica

MARCH 22, 1932–APRIL 27, 2019

D r. Felicisima Serafica, known as Ping, was the first tenured Filipina American professor of psychology in the United States. Her groundbreaking entry into academia as well as her navigation of racism, sexism, and xenophobia are testimony to how women shifted norms and advanced rights over the latter part of the twentieth century and into the twenty-first.

When nineteen-year-old Ping was summoned to the dean's office at the University of the Philippines, she wondered at first if she'd done something wrong. Instead, she discovered she'd been invited to apply for an international scholarship. The University of Pennsylvania had recently welcomed a German scholar; this time, they wanted an Asian student. (In this era, such actions were considered genteel altruism, not tokenism.) Undergrad study abroad was atypical, but Ping's widowed mother had progressive views about women's capabilities. Ping won the

scholarship and enrolled in the school, graduating with a bachelor's degree in psychology in 1952.

Despite an initial embrace from her American hosts, Ping experienced discrimination from the larger American community. In the summer of 1952, before she began graduate school, Ping and the other students in her clinical internship cohort—including an African American student, students from Jamaica and Colombia, and several white young adults—were banned from recreation facilities in Lincoln, Illinois. They were also called names and threatened. In response to this harassment, the students banded together and organized the first local NAACP chapter.

Ping was not a central player in the rights movements of the '60s, but she withstood persistent xenophobia: When the international dominance of the Japanese automotive industry in the 1980s ignited hatred toward any Asian in the US, regardless of origin, she rallied against institutional disdain for intercultural studies and the dearth of opportunities for women in academia. She also lamented the "model minority" myth that caused many Asian Americans to be stereotyped.

In 1956, Ping returned to her homeland and helped establish one of the country's first hospitals for children with developmental disabilities. After a decade there, she returned to the US to earn a doctorate in clinical psychology. She joined the faculty at The Ohio State University, where she remained from 1977 to 2002. Dr. Felicisima "Ping" Serafica was instrumental in advancing the field of developmental psychology as well as advocating for more opportunities and fair treatment for women and Asian people in academia.

In Ping's view, academia provided few chances for women to associate in the workplace. "We rarely saw each other except in the ladies' room occasionally," she said. How can you support women and trans and/or nonbinary people in your life, personally or professionally?

Claudette Colvin

SEPTEMBER 5, 1939–

The backlash to the Emancipation Proclamation and the Reconstruction era was swift and vicious. After the 1896 *Plessy v. Ferguson* ruling codified "separate but equal," African Americans faced discrimination in almost every facet of life, from restaurants and schools to hotels, pools, water fountains—and public transportation. This meant sitting in separate train cars (the ones with broken seats and no heat) and going to the back of the bus.

> "History had me glued to the seat. Harriet Tubman's hands were pushing down on one shoulder and Sojourner Truth's hands were pushing down on the other shoulder. I was paralyzed between these two women, I couldn't move." —C.C.

March 2, 1955, was a normal day in Montgomery, Alabama. A group of energetic teenagers were riding the bus home from school, bantering and joking among themselves, when a white woman boarded the vehicle. The driver ordered the youths to stand up so that the woman could sit down—the entire group would have to move because segregation laws prohibited Black and white people from sitting in the same row. Three of the students obeyed, but Claudette decided to assert the constitutional rights she'd been learning about in class: She'd paid her fare, so she was not giving up her seat.

Outraged that the white woman would have to stand, the driver summoned traffic police. They dragged Claudette off the bus, calling her "a thing" and other, much worse, epithets. By the time they hauled Claudette off to the adult jail, without giving her even a phone call to a loved one, the town was abuzz.

leaders chose an older, more established NAACP secretary with a middle-class appearance, Rosa Parks, to become the plaintiff in the legal test case they were building against the "separate but equal" law. But Claudette had her day in court as plaintiff in the 1956 Supreme Court case *Browder v. Gayle*, which deemed Montgomery's bus segregation unlawful.

After the court victory, Claudette Colvin moved to New York in 1958 and kept a low profile in her adult life. Today, a street in the Bronx is named in honor of the woman who remained seated—and rose in opposition.

Claudette, a minor, did not become the face of the Montgomery bus boycott—instead, local civil rights

Consider exploring bystander intervention training to learn ways to safely support someone who is being unfairly harassed or mistreated. Groups like Right to Be and Operation Respect offer free bystander and conflict de-escalation training.

Lili'uokalani

SEPTEMBER 2, 1838–NOVEMBER 11, 1917

Lydia Lili'u Loloku Walania Wewehi Kamaka'eha (known as Lili'uokalani) was Hawai'i's first and only queen regnant, a woman ruling as a "king" and not just a spouse. Unable to stave off US expansionism and the annexation of Hawai'i, she ruled for only three years.

Born into Hawai'i's royal court, Lili'uokalani was educated at the Royal School with other potential successors to the throne. Her elder brother, David Kalākaua, was elected as heir, and when her younger brother died in 1877, Lili'uokalani became crown princess and next in line.

Some hoped that Queen Emma (see page 118), the widow of Kamehameha IV who was known for her benevolent social work and beloved by the people, would become the next sovereign, but Lili'uokalani proved herself a great leader. When King David went on a world tour in 1881, she served as temporary regent. In this role, she deftly managed the public health crisis caused by a smallpox epidemic. She also represented the Hawaiian royal family in London for Queen Victoria's Golden Jubilee in 1887, and the two monarchs enjoyed a long friendship. When King David died in 1892, Lili'uokalani ascended to the throne.

Meanwhile, settlers and plantation owners had been deceiving and pressuring the Hawaiian monarchs into signing away most of their power over the course of a century. As queen, Lili'uokalani tried to maintain the monarchy, but Hawai'i was coveted for both its geopolitical position and its sugarcane. After the Spanish-American War, the US government became wholly invested in expanding its territory. In 1893, the monarchy slipped away, beginning with a staged coup led by the Dole family and the US Marines and ending

"The cause of Hawaiian independence is larger and dearer than the life of any man connected with it." —L.

when the US declared the Hawaiian Islands a protectorate.

Two years later, Lili'uokalani was placed under house arrest. She officially abdicated her throne and was exiled to the mainland, where she composed music and wrote her memoir: *Hawaii's Story by Hawaii's Queen*, the only autobiography written by a Hawaiian monarch.

Though Lili'uokalani's efforts to maintain Hawai'i's autonomy were ultimately unsuccessful (the Islands were formally annexed by the United States on July 12, 1898, and Hawai'i became the fiftieth state on August 21, 1959), she is still revered as a local heroine.

If you were queen, what food would you want at your coronation banquet? Create the menu, and if you can, choose one of the dishes to prepare for yourself or with others.

Mamie "Peanut" Johnson

SEPTEMBER 27, 1935–DECEMBER 18, 2017

When Major League Baseball finally admitted the Negro Leagues' players, statistics, and records into their official annals in 2020, many rejoiced that superstars like Satchel Paige, Josh Gibson, and Cool Papa Bell would finally get the honor they were due. Three women players are also gaining more recognition for smashing the glass diamond: second base players Toni Stone and Connie Morgan and pitcher Mamie "Peanut" Johnson, all members of the Indianapolis Clowns. (At five foot three, Mamie got her nickname when an opposing batter underestimated her, saying she shouldn't be on the pitcher's mound because she "wasn't any bigger than a peanut." She silenced him by promptly striking him out.)

Born in South Carolina, Mamie learned an improvisatory form of baseball from a relative: Tree branches were the bats, rocks wrapped in tape were the balls, and pie plates stood in for bases. In 1945, when she was living with relatives in Long Branch, New Jersey, she made an all-white boys Police Athletic Club team. As the only Black person and the only girl on the squad, Mamie was often

> "I can get rowdy, too. That's no problem. I met some of the nicest gentlemen I could ever meet and I got the highest respect in the world from all of them." —M.J.

teased and hassled—but that razzing stopped after she helped carry the team to two division championships.

Later, Mamie moved to Washington, DC, where she reunited with her mother and joined two local semipro "sandlot" Black men's teams.

By age eighteen, she'd learned how to combine her strong right arm and her baseball brain. That same year, a scout for the Clowns invited her to try out for the team; she nabbed a place on the squad the next day.

This was a vindication since Mamie had been denied even a tryout with the All-American Girls Professional Baseball League because of the color line the year before. Mamie "Peanut" Johnson later called this a blessing in disguise because she found playing alongside men to be so satisfying. No doubt—the legendary Satchel Paige helped her perfect her curveball.

Mamie Johnson pitched three seasons with the Clowns, holding a lifetime record of 33–8, a .805 winning percentage, which is Hall of Fame material! Build your own Hall of Fame for a sport or hobby or activity you love. Who are your first ten inductees?

Alice Moore Dunbar-Nelson

JULY 19, 1875–SEPTEMBER 18, 1935

Alice Moore Dunbar-Nelson's lifetime coincided with the emergence of new realities around race, gender, sexuality, and literature. Indeed, the progression of names she wrote under in the early twentieth century (Alice Ruth Moore, Alice Dunbar, Mrs. Paul Dunbar, Alice Moore Dunbar, Alice Dunbar Nelson, Aliceruth Dunbar-Nelson, and Alice Ruth Moore Dunbar, among others) demonstrates that as society moved from the Reconstruction era to the Harlem Renaissance, women endeavored to control how they expressed themselves and their identities.

A light-skinned, middle-class, multiracial Creole woman in New Orleans, Alice enjoyed a certain privilege, publishing her first book, *Violets and Other Tales*, a collection of short prose and poetry at once classical and experimental, at age twenty. The celebrated poet Paul Laurence Dunbar fell in love with her after seeing a photo of her that accompanied one of her stories in a newspaper clipping; during their two-year-long letter-writing romance, they fashioned themselves an American version of another epistolary couple, Robert and Elizabeth Barrett Browning. After their wedding in 1898, Paul, who had already revealed himself as abusive during their courtship, became ever more so;

Alice left him in 1902, returning his desperate pleas for reunion with a one-word telegram: *No.*

Alice devoted herself to teaching at a high school in Delaware and crafting keen observations and critiques of American society through her writing: four novels, two volumes of oratory, poetry, short stories, dramas, essays, and newspaper articles and reviews. She was also politically active, working as a field organizer for the women's suffragist movement and delivering essays and speeches against lynching.

She also liberated herself in her personal life: According to her diaries, she enjoyed love affairs with women for years (historians surmise that jealousy and revulsion over this fact was one of the reasons Paul was abusive), but she also loved men. In 1910, she married a work colleague, Henry A. Callis, but the relationship was short-lived. In 1916, she finally found stability in her marriage to journalist and activist Robert J. Nelson.

Alice understood that art and action were intertwined. She wrote plays as much for literature's sake as to give her students a chance to perform and find their own identities beyond the "blonde ideal of beauty to worship . . . milk-white literature to assimilate, and . . . pearly Paradise to anticipate, in which their dark faces would be hopelessly out of place."

For many years after her death at age sixty in 1935, Alice Moore Dunbar-Nelson's legacy remained buried. Her diary, a compelling chronicle of the highs and lows that an African American woman experienced during the Harlem Renaissance era, wasn't published until 1984. The publication led to a posthumous appreciation of her vast body of writing and the conviction with which she wrote about the changing world and her place in it.

Organize a reading of Alice's poetry (or that of another feminist poet) with a few friends. Take turns reading her words aloud and end with a discussion about her life and work. What surprises, inspires, confuses, intrigues, angers, and delights you?

Lozen

1840–1889

Chihenne Chiricahua Apache warrior Lozen had many gifts: skill with horses, healing powers as a medicine woman and midwife, fearlessness in battle, and a preternatural ability to divine the strategic mind and moves of the enemy. Even as a child, she preferred the art of war over domestic tasks.

Highly skilled, stealthy, and bold warriors, the seminomadic Apache were one of the last tribes to succumb to American subjugation. They had already resisted Mexican dominance of their territory—the Mexicans placed a bounty on the tribe, literally paying a fee for the black hair and scalp of any man, woman, or child—and were equally motivated to resist the American cavalry, which sought to seize Apache land, livestock, and

> ## "Strong as a man, braver than most, and cunning in strategy, Lozen is a shield to her people."
>
> —Victorio, Lozen's brother

mineral riches for expansionist settlers, plunderers, and Gold Rush travelers.

The strain of war and deprivation proved devastating for the Apache, whose impoverished reservation lands were called "Hell's Forty Acres." Between 1877 and 1880, Lozen and her brother, chief and warrior Victorio, were part of the running battle with first the Mexican and then the Anglo armies. Victorio referred to his brazen sister as his right hand.

Lozen is known for many heroic actions, some apocryphal and others documented through oral history:

She rode her horse through a hail of gunfire; delivered a baby in the middle of the desert while fleeing the cavalry; crossed a rushing river on horseback to lead the women and children of the tribe to safety before returning to the battle on the other side; swiped munitions with impunity; and stole horses so easily that one might have thought she and the beasts shared an understanding.

Lozen also had a special connection to Ussen, an Apache deity who, it is said, gave her the vision to know what the enemy was going to do and when they would strike. After Victorio met his demise at the 1880 Battle of Tres Castillos, Lozen joined the band of Apache leader Geronimo. She fought on until 1886, when she was captured as a prisoner of war; she ultimately died from tuberculosis in 1889.

Lozen had a sixth sense about horses and used this to her advantage in defending her people. What do you consider to be one of your superpowers? How has it helped you?

Clara Brown

CA. 1800–OCTOBER 26, 1885

D uring the era of American slavery, it was common for enslaved people to be treated like chattel or machines; if enslavers could make more money selling their "property" to another speculator, they would break up families with no remorse. When this terrible fate befell Clara Brown, she never gave up on her quest to find her daughter Eliza Jane. Even after Clara was technically freed from slavery, she worked as a domestic for a family. When the patriarch, a Mormon, decided to relocate the family west, Clara was banned from riding in the wagon train and forced to walk the entire seven-hundred-mile trip from Kansas to Denver. Yet she never lost hope of finding her daughter, even after she reportedly became the first Black settler in Gold Rush Colorado.

She believed in God, and she believed in Eliza Jane.

Clara's work ethic served her well in the pioneer setting. She became Central City, Colorado's first laundress—no glamorous task in a town of single, gritty miners. She was considered to be Colorado's first midwife, a cook, a caretaker, a nurse, and—as her wealth grew—a philanthropist and the nineteenth-century version of a venture capitalist. Aunt Clara, as she was known, lent speculators money for mining equipment in exchange for future profits. She eventually earned enough to purchase property and helped establish several churches.

After Emancipation, Clara returned to Kentucky and Tennessee, still searching for Eliza Jane. Though she didn't find her daughter, she brought Freedmen back west with her, supporting them morally, physically, and financially. Her efforts helped establish the Black Mountain West community.

By 1882, Clara was in an unfortunate state, having endured fires and floods that damaged her home and eviscerated her savings as well as years of hard domestic labor that left her in poor health. Nevertheless, when she learned from other travelers that her child was likely alive, her determination was rekindled. The community took up a collection to help the now penniless

octogenarian buy a train ticket to Iowa. Her reunion with Eliza Jane, now a mother herself, made local news with the headline "Mother and Daughter United After a Separation of Thirty Years." The family enjoyed many visits over the final three years of Clara's life.

A stained-glass window at the Colorado State Capitol building and a contemporary opera about her life are but two of the many tributes to Clara Brown, the "Angel of the Rockies."

> **"The kind old friend whose heart always responded to the cry of distress, and who, rising from the humble position of slave to the angelic type of noble woman, won our sympathy and commanded our respect."**
>
> —Words spoken at Clara Brown's funeral

Reach out to a loved one, whether that means calling a relative, walking or hiking with a good friend, or some other way of deeply connecting with a person, a pet, or even a cherished memory.

Alice Augusta Ball

JULY 24, 1892–DECEMBER 31, 1916

A lice Augusta Ball was born in the Pacific Northwest during a time when lighter-skinned Black people could access certain privileges of middle-class life. Both of her parents were photographers, and her grandfather was among the first Black Americans to use daguerreotype (a process that combined chemicals on metal plates to create photographs), which was a revolutionary innovation at the time.

Alice earned bachelor's degrees in chemistry and pharmacy, even publishing a paper in the *Journal of the American Chemical Society* as an undergraduate—a rarity for a woman. In 1915, she became the first African American and the first woman to earn a master of science in chemistry from

the University of Hawai'i. But her biggest contribution to medicine was yet to come.

Hansen's disease, formerly known as leprosy, was once one of the world's most dreaded diseases. With no pragmatic treatment, those stricken with the bacterial infection were banished to leper colonies, such as Moloka'i Island in Hawai'i, to live out their days in exile and pain. Soon after getting her master's degree, Alice introduced a groundbreaking innovation to treat leprosy: The oil of the tropical chaulmoogra plant, while effective, was too thick to inject and too noxious to ingest, so Alice discovered a way to isolate the oil into an injectable solvent. What later became known as the Ball Method was used to successfully treat leprosy patients until new medicines emerged in the 1940s.

Tragically, Alice died at the age of twenty-four, most likely from

> "The annals of medical science are incomplete unless full credit is given for the work of Alice Ball. . . . Miss Ball won the fight for others."
>
> —American Missionary Association, April 1922

inhaling chemical poisons while teaching in a lab. Her work was not lost to history, but rather stolen by a white male colleague who put his name on her research papers, claimed credit for her discovery, and commercialized the treatment. It was not until 2000 that intrepid researchers connected the dots and helped restore her honor.

Today, the University of Hawai'i awards a scholarship in recognition of scientific pioneer Alice Augusta Ball, the school's first African American chemistry instructor and researcher.

If you could create a cure for any disease, which one would it be and why?

Susan La Flesche Picotte

JUNE 17, 1865–SEPTEMBER 18, 1915

W hen Susan La Flesche was eight years old, she saw a sick woman die as a result of negligence and discrimination: Even though a messenger sent for a doctor four times, medical professionals never showed up for "just" an Indian. Few in her Omaha tribe were surprised. Native Americans had already suffered three hundred years of decimation, from European diseases that wiped out entire tribes to forced migration, territorial wars, and physical constraints on reservations with inferior resources and minimal self-determination. As the first Native American doctor in the US, Susan dedicated her life to improving the welfare of her people.

"We who are educated have to be pioneers of Indian civilization. The white people have reached a high standard of civilization, but how many years has it taken them? We are only beginning; so do not try to put us down, but help us to climb higher. Give us a chance."

—S.L.P.

While some elders held on to traditions like buffalo hunts and powwows, children like Susan were encouraged to learn European history and values. After attending reservation school and an East Coast boarding school, Susan went to the Hampton Normal and Agricultural Institute, a Black college that also admitted Native Americans, in faraway Virginia. She graduated second in her class in 1886. Three years later, thanks to a network of progressive patrons, she earned a degree from the Woman's

Medical College of Pennsylvania, one of the nation's few medical schools for women.

As a new doctor, she was given a very arduous post back on the Omaha Reservation: She would be the lone doctor covering more than 1,350 square miles. Dr. Sue, as she was called, worked tirelessly to heal and treat the sick. She encouraged public hygiene to help prevent communicable and incurable diseases like tuberculosis and cholera. Alcoholism was also destroying lives and families on the reservation—her own husband later succumbed to alcohol-related tuberculosis—so she advocated for temperance.

Susan's patients sometimes resisted Western medicine, so she incorporated traditional healing into her treatments. As the community grew to trust and rely on her, she was asked to provide legal advice, emotional support and counseling, and even assistance navigating the draconian bureaucracy of the Bureau of Indian Affairs. Others simply used her office as a quiet place to rest. Even after working twenty-hour days, Susan kept a lantern lit in her window so sick patients could find her house at any hour of the day or night, even in a snowstorm.

Susan La Flesche Picotte's dream was to build a local hospital, a feat she accomplished in 1913, two years before her death at age fifty. It was the first privately funded hospital on a reservation.

If you were an architect or municipal planner, what community or city building or structure would you most like to build, and why?

Catarina de San Juan

CA. 1607–JANUARY 5, 1688

Whether you have Mexican roots, have eaten in a Mexican restaurant, or have even bought a condiment considered Mexican, you've probably seen la china poblana, the traditional dress style of Mexican women. But you might not know that this cultural archetype was actually inspired by a real person.

Penned by a Jesuit priest, the longest book to come out of the Spanish colonial era is the three-volume account of the life of Catarina de San Juan. From this book, oral histories, and other religious writings of the period, we learn of this woman's remarkable and adventuresome (although perhaps not entirely historically accurate) life. As a young girl, Mira (her name at the time) was kidnapped by Portuguese pirates. They dropped her off at the Indian port city of Cochin (known today as Kochi), where she converted to Catholicism. She was later sold to Spanish traffickers in the port of Manila. The Spaniards planned to ship her off as a palace servant to the viceroy of Mexico, but when she arrived in Acapulco, she was instead sold to a man named Miguel de Sosa and given the Christian name Catarina de San Juan.

Living in the city of Puebla, Catarina worked for the de Sosas until they both passed away, at which point she married the Chinese servant of a local priest. Her husband's heritage, plus the fact that all Asians in Mexico were called Chinese no matter which region or country they came from, perhaps contributed to Catarina's nickname, La China.

Though Catarina was an extremely devout Catholic and even experienced visions of the Virgin Mary and Baby Jesus, marriage disqualified her from fulfilling her dream of entering the convent. Instead, she became a beata—the designation the Catholic Church gives to a woman who has received a heavenly blessing.

While in Puebla, Catarina de San Juan never stopped wearing the Indian sari of her childhood. Over the years, she added a petticoat to the frock, and the style became popular among the women of Puebla and later Mexico City—they added a low-cut embroidered white blouse (scandalous for the time), sometimes with a kerchief tied in for modesty, and a billowing skirt decorated with sequins and shells. Eventually, the design incorporated the Mexican coat of arms—an eagle clutching a snake and a prickly pear cactus—and became the national costume of Mexico.

The china poblana costume is still worn today on both sides of the border. What do you like to wear to demonstrate your cultural history? Draw a sketch of it.

Kala Bagai

CA. 1892–1983

....

Born in Amritsar, India, Kala Bagai was in her early twenties when she and her husband, Vaishno, arrived at Angel Island in San Francisco Bay in 1915. With modest savings and young kids in tow, they were determined to build a new life in the Bay Area. But at the time, there were barely two thousand South Asians in the United States, and xenophobia against Chinese and South Asian people was rampant. Neighbors barricaded them from entering the house they had purchased in Berkeley, forcing them to move their family and small store across the Bay to San Francisco.

Although the US census categorized South Asians as members of the "Caucasoid race" and some high-caste Hindus were naturalized as "free white people," the Supreme Court's 1923 ruling in *United States v. Bhagat Singh Thind* broadly disqualified Asian Indians from citizenship because they were not visibly "white." This ruling stripped Vaishno of his newly bestowed American citizenship, and in protest and anguish, he ended his life.

After her husband's death, Kala moved to Los Angeles, married a platonic family friend, attended night school while raising her three sons, and generously opened her home to new arrivals from all parts of India. The environment she created for her compatriots was so welcoming that the community began calling her "Mother India." Finally, with the passage of the Luce-Celler Act in 1946, she was able to attain US citizenship. Kala lived out her years surrounded by family and friends.

It was not until Kala's granddaughter Rani Bagai was going through family papers that she learned of her amazing foremother. Thanks to Rani's advocacy, the city of Berkeley named a two-block stretch of downtown Kala Bagai Way in honor of this generous and resilient woman. Designated in 2020, it became the third street in the United States to be named after a South Asian woman (the other two streets are named in honor of Kalpana Chawla—see page 26).

Host a dinner party, brunch, picnic, or potluck for a handful of people you know, or meet a friend for tea or coffee. How does enjoying food and drink enhance your time together?

Marie Laveau

SEPTEMBER 10, 1801–JUNE 15, 1881

A nyone who's traveled to New Orleans has likely encountered souvenirs emblazoned with the image of Marie Laveau, the "Voodoo Queen of New Orleans." Her name and legend have inspired so much lore and admiration and also so much fear and speculation that it can be difficult to separate her real story from the superstition that surrounds it.

We do know she was a descendant of French colonialists, enslaved Black people, Choctaw Indians, and free Creoles of color. Her first husband, Jacques Paris, was part of the mass immigration to southern Louisiana after the Haitian Revolution (the only successful uprising of Black people in the Americas). Over time, he and their two daughters disappeared from the historical record. Marie entered into a common-law marriage

with a wealthy white man of French noble descent and they had children together, although it's unclear how many.

Marie lived in a New Orleans still governed by the old Code Noir (Black Rules), which allowed Black and Native Americans to gather freely only on Sundays and holidays. She and her community would congregate around Congo Square—the birthplace of jazz—to socialize, garden, and sell wares. She sold gris-gris (amulet bags filled with herbs, a vestige of West African healing arts) to those seeking remedies for ailments both physical and spiritual. It's likely Marie also worked as a hairdresser to wealthy white New Orleanian women, becoming their trusted confidant.

She was also a healer, commingling the rites of Papal Catholicism with traditional African dances, drumming, and rootwork. Though she was an old woman during the yellow fever outbreak of 1878, she attended to the needs of the stricken, and it is even said that she occasionally ministered to prisoners on death row.

A talented singer and dancer, Marie often led festivities such as Lake Pontchartrain's annual St. John's Eve celebrations. This event had solstice traditions such as bonfires and singing, and Haitian rituals such as drumming and conjuring of the spirits—a mix of Old European pagan practice and African diasporic rites. Marie's performance skills as well as her gift for the healing arts earned her the nickname of Voodoo Queen. The rest of Marie's life and history are unknown.

Conjecture and tourist-trap lore aside, perhaps Marie Laveau should be most celebrated for being a self-determined community leader and a keeper of woman-centered spirituality.

What are some traditional and/or cultural healing or self-care methods that interest you? How might you begin practicing them?

Marsha P. Johnson

AUGUST 24, 1945–JULY 6, 1992

One day in 1963, a high school graduate boarded a train in Elizabeth, New Jersey, with just fifteen dollars. Over the course of the one-hour trip to New York, clothing was changed and mannerisms were transformed. The young adult disembarked as her authentic self: Black Marsha.

New York City's Greenwich Village was a longtime safe haven for truth seekers, wanderers, and outcasts, and a 1966 ruling that allowed gay bars to legally serve alcohol boosted the party spirit. Marsha soon found employment as a server in a Greenwich Village restaurant and dove into the downtown drag scene. Andy Warhol himself photographed her drag performance squad, the Hot Peaches, for a 1975 Polaroid portrait exhibit entitled *Ladies and Gentlemen*. All the same, dancing in public with someone of the same gender (not to mention kissing, holding hands, or having sex) remained illegal, and for marginalized groups, sex work was often the only means of survival. Marsha, who sourced many of her grandiose outfits

from garbage bins, was arrested more than one hundred times—sometimes for engaging in sex work and other times for simply walking down Forty-Second Street in drag.

Such was the backdrop for the NYPD raid at the Stonewall Inn on June 28, 1969. The police were always raiding the bars, but on this night, the patrons fought back. Marsha (who had by now adopted the last name Johnson, after the Howard Johnson's diner on the Greenwich Village corner where the drag queens often hung out) arrived at a scene that had devolved into a full-out riot. Black, poor, gay, and unapologetic, she jumped right in. It is said that she shimmied up a light pole with a heavy object in her purse, which she sent crashing down on a squad car.

While America's LGBTQIA+ rights movement began that night, the real work lay ahead. In 1970, Marsha created Street Transvestite Action Revolutionaries (STAR) with friend and fellow trans rights activist Sylvia Rivera (see page 160). STAR

(see page 160)

> ## "Darling, I want my gay rights now!"
> —M.P.J.

served as the first LGBTQIA+ youth shelter in the US and hosted meetings where trans activists and their supporters planned demonstrations. Despite this positive impact, Marsha endured abusive clients, police harassment, an HIV diagnosis, and many periods of incarceration—sometimes in jails, sometimes at Bellevue Hospital due to undiagnosed schizophrenia. In 1992, days after the New York Pride parade, her body was found floating in the Hudson River. The official ruling—suicide—was later changed to possible homicide.

Nicknamed the "Mayor of Christopher Street," Marsha was a pioneering force for gay and trans rights, and her legacy continues today. In 2020, East River State Park, located on the site of a former shipping dock in Williamsburg, Brooklyn, was renamed Marsha P. Johnson State Park.

When a judge asked Marsha what the *P* in her name stood for, she said, "Pay it no mind." Come up with an empowering phrase inspired by your first or middle initial.

Emma Ping Lum

AUGUST 10, 1910–MAY 29, 1989

Born into a politically active family, Emma Ping Lum had a sense of fairness and justice instilled in her from a young age. Her father, Walter U. Lum, was an influential member of San Francisco's Chinese community and editor of the *Chinese Times* newspaper, which he launched in 1924. As founder of the Chinese American Citizens Alliance, he and his wife raised their seven children in a household full of discussion and debate. A recurring topic was how to abolish the Expatriation Act of 1907 and the Chinese Exclusion Act of 1882—xenophobic laws that greatly restricted emigration from China and undermined the stability and prosperity of Chinese Americans and their second-generation children.

Despite the racial hostility and inferior educational environments Asians experienced in the US at this time, Emma excelled in academics: first in high school; then at San Francisco State College, where she earned her BA; then at Columbia University, where she received a master's degree. Her advanced education and her fluency in several Chinese dialects proved useful when she began working at the San Francisco Office of Censorship in 1943 during World War II. Her role involved scrutinizing mail and cables for potentially subversive and dangerous messages, and she was awarded a Certificate of Merit for her efforts. After the war, she attended San Francisco's UC Hastings College of the Law. Upon passing the bar exam in 1947, Emma became the first Chinese American woman attorney in the United States and, in 1952, the first Chinese American woman to practice before the US Supreme Court.

In her private practice, she served both Asian and Anglo clientele, but her primary focus was on immigration law. She also employed her sister as her secretary during her forty-two years at the firm. A happy, single, child-free

working woman, Emma Ping Lum used the law to build on her family's progressive values. She also enjoyed traveling to places like Cuba, Europe, and the Hawaiian Islands, a favorite destination.

Emma once stated in an interview that she loved her job, including its long hours and hard work, but also enjoyed hobbies such as horseback riding, boating, bicycling, and dancing. If you could go on any vacay, where would you go and what activities would you do? Create your dream itinerary!

Mary Fields

CA. 1832–DECEMBER 5, 1914

Mary Fields stood six feet tall by the age of eighteen, and she was physically stronger than many of the men in her Tennessee village. Once the Emancipation Proclamation freed her and other enslaved people, she sought a new life as a housekeeper at a Toledo, Ohio, convent, where a friend had become the Mother Superior. When her friend headed to a convent in the less settled lands of Montana, Mary decided to follow.

Although she enjoyed her job of doing laundry and maintaining the grounds and gardens at the convent, Mary's saloon-loving, gun-toting, fiery ways were not convent-appropriate—but even the nuns knew better than to cross her. When a local cowpoke insulted Mary in 1894 because she ("an uppity colored woman") outearned him, they got into a heated shoot-out behind the nunnery; blood was shed, though neither was gravely injured. Nevertheless, the regional bishop deemed such behavior misaligned with the convent's moral code, and he dismissed Mary from the nunnery.

She tried her hand at a few other occupations before she applied for and secured a competitive contract with the United States Postal Service to be a Star Route carrier. (It is said she won the contract because of the speed with which she could hitch a team of horses.) The fifteen-mile rural route was hers. At age sixty-three, she learned to drive a tonne-weight horse-drawn stagecoach over the rocky Montana terrain. Later known as Stagecoach Mary, she relied on her rifle and no-nonsense attitude to overcome the harsh climate, highway bandits, and a memorable encounter with wolves. She held down the route for eight years, not only gaining a reputation as a reliable mail carrier but also connecting remote homes across the Western plains.

Mary challenged society's confines of gender by smoking cigars, wearing men's clothes, and even serving as the local baseball team's mascot. After retiring from the mail service, she remained a beloved community member, running a laundromat and providing childcare for local families. When she passed away in 1914, Stagecoach Mary received one of the biggest funerals the town of Cascade, Montana, had ever seen.

Fun fact: February 4 is National Thank a Mail Carrier Day! Do you know your mail carriers or others who provide a regular, essential service that you might take for granted? How can you connect with them and show your appreciation?

Old Elizabeth

CA. 1765–1866

Elizabeth, author of the 1863 book *Memoir of Old Elizabeth, a Coloured Woman*, was born into slavery in Maryland around 1765. As was the practice, she was given neither a last name nor formal instruction in reading and writing, yet hers is one of the oldest preserved narratives by an enslaved woman of the antebellum years.

Elizabeth was about eleven when she experienced the trauma of being sold to another family. Desperate to see her mother, she asked the new owner to let her visit; unsurprisingly, he refused. Her desire was so strong, however, that she defied the owner and walked the twenty or so miles to the old farm. Upon her return to the new plantation, she was soundly whipped. Her suffering and its aftermath propelled her into a severe state of emotional and mental distress. At its height, Elizabeth's agony transmuted into a celestial vision, which she considered her call to the ministry.

Elizabeth was eventually sold to a Presbyterian minister, who liberated her at age thirty. She wished to become a traveling minister, but as her vision had forewarned, Elizabeth was rejected and mocked for being a woman. She could not read, but she could preach, and while the official Presbyterian Church didn't approve, she officiated in-home prayer meetings, eventually traveling around the mid-Atlantic, upper Midwest, and even Canada to share the gospel. Her message deeply affected the hearts of her audience, leading some adherents to even offer payment:

One [white audience member], a great scripturian, fixed himself behind the door with pen and ink, in order to take down the discourse in short-hand; but the Almighty Being anointed me with such a portion of his Spirit, that he cast away his paper and pen, and heard the discourse with patience, and was much affected, for the Lord wrought powerfully on his heart. After meeting, he came forward and offered me his hand with solemnity on his countenance, and handed me something to pay for my conveyance home.

After living in Michigan, Elizabeth moved to Philadelphia at age eighty-seven. Under the name Old Elizabeth, she began to dictate her memoir ten years later.

In her memoir, Elizabeth describes how audiences both Black and white would gather to hear her preach: "Many no doubt from curiosity to hear what the old coloured woman had to say." Who is the most memorable speaker you've ever heard and what did you find inspiring about them?

Lydia Mendoza

MAY 31, 1916–DECEMBER 20, 2007

Tejano music pioneer Lydia Mendoza was a musical storyteller for her people. With a voice both crystalline and robust, she stood alone on the stage with an unconventionally tuned twelve-string guitar, and for a while, she was one of the most famous performing artists on either side of the border. Her legacy paved the way for a number of singers, from Linda Ronstadt to Selena Quintanilla-Pérez.

The Tejano trace their roots to Spanish, Mexican, and Indigenous peoples, sharing foodways, traditions, language, and music. One can often detect Spanish and Mexican folk, Cajun, and vaquero (cowboy) music in Tejano songs, along with smatterings of rock 'n' roll, country, and the polka of the German, Czech, and Polish populations that migrated to Texas during the 1830s.

Lydia's parents were part of the mass exodus of Mexicans fleeing the revolution. They landed in Houston, where their young daughter learned to sing by imitating her mother and aunt. Her family initially worked as farm laborers but found music to be more lucrative: By the time Lydia was eleven, they'd formed a family band, Cuarteto Carta Blanca. Labels at the time were seeking non-English acts to round out their "race music" catalogs, and the Mendozas were signed in 1928. While the family enjoyed some success, it was Lydia who was discovered by a local Spanish-language radio host and given a spot on his program. As the public came to know and love her talent, she found herself embarking on a solo career.

Like many blues artists of the 1930s and '40s, Lydia performed songs about hard times and real life, suffered under the racist conventions of the Jim Crow/Juan Crow era, and endured an exploitative record label. When Lydia recorded her signature

> "It doesn't matter if it's a corrido, a waltz, a bolero, a polka or whatever. When I sing that song, I live that song." —L.M.

song "Mal Hombre" in 1934, she didn't know how to read or write in either English or Spanish, so she signed away her royalties to Bluebird Records for a mere fifteen dollars.

Despite this mishap, she enjoyed a career that spanned six decades, fifty albums, and more than two hundred songs. In 1982, Lydia Mendoza became the first Texan to be named a National Heritage Fellow by the National Endowment for the Arts, and she was inducted into the Texas Women's Hall of Fame in 1985. In 2013, she was even enshrined on a US postage stamp as an ode to her great musical contributions.

In addition to being known as the "Lark of the Border," Lydia was celebrated as the "cancionera del barrio," or singer of the everyday folk. If you were (or are!) a singer, what song would you perform to celebrate your favorite she-roes?

Florynce "Flo" Kennedy

FEBRUARY 11, 1916–DECEMBER 21, 2000

In the 1940s, educated women were expected to be schoolteachers, but Florynce "Flo" Kennedy wanted to change laws. The daughter of a man who once chased a band of threatening Klansmen from the family's front porch, she was not one to back away from a challenge. An example: When Columbia Law School denied her admission

because of her gender, she threatened to sue. The school let her in, and she graduated in 1951— one of eight women in her class, and the only Black woman.

After graduation, Flo started her own firm. She represented Black activists and revolutionaries, defended the estates of jazz legends Billie Holiday and Charlie Parker from greedy record companies, and even sued the Roman Catholic Church for overreaching its tax-exempt status by involving itself in antiabortion activism.

Yet the work was underpaid and frustrating. The court of law was not a potent-enough venue for ending oppression. "When you want to get to the suites, start in the streets," she was known to say.

Flo had a rapier wit as well as one of the loudest moral bullhorns of the 1970s. Whether she was organizing a boycott against advertising agencies that excluded Black people from their campaigns, participating in rallies against the Vietnam War or in support of reproductive rights, or cofounding both the Feminist Party (which supported Democratic presidential candidate Shirley Chisholm; see page 20) and the National Women's Political Caucus in 1971, Flo was a prime mover. She even found time to do some TV and movie acting.

Although she founded the National Black Feminist Organization in 1973, Flo disagreed with racial

page 20

"Don't agonize, organize." —F.K.

division in feminism; she believed it diluted the cause. Her double billing with feminist legend Gloria Steinem (the pair later dubbed themselves "the Thelma and Louise of the '70s") made them favorites on the college speaking circuit. Sometimes the campuses were also sites of protest, such as the massive 1973 "pee-in" Flo helped stage on the grounds of Harvard University to protest the scarcity of women's restrooms.

In addition to her great achievements, Florynce "Flo" Kennedy is remembered for her signature look (a cowboy hat and pink sunglasses), her ribald sense of humor, and her supremely quotable quotes, including "If men could get pregnant, abortion would be a sacrament."

One of Flo's most famous quotes is
"Freedom is like taking a bath:
You got to keep doing it every day."
What is a daily practice you can take up
to add more strength and purpose to your life?

Umeko Tsuda

DECEMBER 31, 1864–AUGUST 16, 1929

Seeking international influences to help modernize Japan, the Meiji Imperial dynasty sent five young girls to the United States to learn about American life and culture in 1871. The youngest of the group was six-year-old Umeko (also known as Ume) Tsuda, whose achievements as an educator and feminist resonate to this day.

In Washington, DC, Umeko boarded with an American statesman and his wife, a childless couple who doted on their "sunbeam from the land of the rising sun." She adapted well to America, converting to Christianity and graduating from high school with prizes in writing and deportment, among other honors. In fact, when she returned to Tokyo in 1882, she barely remembered Japanese and had trouble using chopsticks.

Back in Japan, Umeko yearned to be more than a tutor, even though it was considered a somewhat prestigious assignment. As the women's suffrage movement gathered momentum in the US and elsewhere, Umeko questioned Japan's traditional patriarchy. She believed that girls should learn more than how to be good homemakers and wives; they deserved a liberal arts education and the ability to choose their career and make their own money.

In 1889, she returned to the US, matriculating at Philadelphia's Bryn Mawr College. Determined to help other Japanese women study abroad,

"Do not worry about me, dear Mrs. Lannan. . . . I am in such a happy home. . . . Though I may find it hard to get accustomed to many things and often feel strange and lonely, I have so many blessings and so many friends . . . that soon I shall feel that this is my own home and America only a preparing place."

—U.T., *The Attic Letters: Ume Tsuda's Correspondence to Her American Mother*

she raised $8,000 (about $240,000 today) to establish the American Women's Scholarship for Japanese Women, which sponsored twenty-five Japanese women before it ended in 1976.

After taking graduate courses at the University of Oxford in England, Umeko returned once more to Japan. Convinced that educated women would improve Japanese society, she enlisted her American and Japanese friends to help her establish a liberal arts school for women. In 1900, Umeko founded Tokyo's Joshi Eigaku Juku (Women's Institute for English Studies), which admitted students regardless of social status—another nod to the growing progressivism of the West. Today, the highly prestigious Tsuda University is one of Japan's oldest higher-education institutions for women, and in 2019, the Bank of Japan announced a forthcoming ¥5,000 banknote featuring Umeko Tsuda's portrait.

Umeko depended on a network of friends to help realize her dreams. Who is someone in your life you turn to for encouragement and support? Send them a postcard, a bouquet of flowers, or another token of gratitude to let them know how much you love them.

Etel Adnan

FEBRUARY 24, 1925–NOVEMBER 14, 2021

Lebanese American poet and multimedia artist Etel Adnan spent her entire life both embodying and rejecting the confines of geopolitical boundaries, as well as redefining what personal and creative identity can be.

A painter, feminist and lesbian, war chronicler and memoirist, and one of the most accomplished Arab American authors, Etel was born in 1925 in Beirut, Lebanon, just as the nation was gaining independent statehood. The child of a Greek Orthodox mother and a Muslim Turkish Syrian father, she noticed that while she was speaking Greek, Turkish, and French in her private school, the majority of people around her were speaking Arabic, a language she would never fully master. This tension between language, identity, class, nation, and destiny ended up being an important theme in Etel's visual art and writing alike: She decorated leporellos—giant books folded in an accordion style—with abstractions of color and Arabic writing, uniting the two parts of her creative identity.

Though Etel Adnan did not gain wide recognition as a visual artist until she was in her late eighties, she was renowned for decades as a poet and novelist, detailing and decrying the brutality and chaos of the 1970s Lebanese Civil War and other Middle East conflicts. For someone who called many places home—the provisional nation-state of Lebanon in childhood; Paris for her university years; Berkeley, California, and Cambridge, Massachusetts, for grad school

> **"Abstract art was the equivalent of poetic expression; I didn't need to use words, but colors and lines. I didn't need to belong to a language-oriented culture but to an open form of expression."** —E.A.

at Harvard in the counterculture 1960s; and later, Paris again, by way of Bahrain and Marrakesh—this nonagenarian was a true citizen of the world, yet one who considered herself an outsider in exile and who refused to be limited by borders, boundaries, or labels.

How does your birthplace or where you grew up define who you are and how you live and think? Draw a map of what feels like your "chosen homeland." Add your home base, your happy place, your secret hideaway, your safety spot, and so on.

Martha Louise Morrow Foxx

OCTOBER 9, 1902–SEPTEMBER 1985

Though Martha Louise Morrow Foxx lost most of her vision during infancy, neither she nor her parents expected her dreams to diminish. Born in North Carolina and raised in Philadelphia, Martha was well aware of the deprivation that sharecroppers and other descendants of enslaved people suffered. She enrolled at Temple University in 1927, and after her first year there, she was offered a role as teacher and principal at the new Mississippi Blind School for Negroes at the Piney Woods School in rural Rankin County.

The Piney Woods School was founded in 1909 with little more than a Bible and the determination of a man named Laurence Clifton Jones to redress the county's 80 percent illiteracy level. Mississippi's

difficult agricultural conditions, including punishing heat and poor soil, contributed to a high poverty level, and the rise of racist hate crimes in the South made it a dangerous place to try to advocate for African American advancement. Martha was dedicated to the call and applied herself to teaching and providing round-the-clock care for ten blind students. "She ministered, not only to their intellectual needs, but to their moral and spiritual needs as well. She developed self-reliance in all of her students so that they could eagerly look forward to the time when they could support themselves out in the world," said Jones.

Martha developed a rigorous early form of experimental education: foraging wild berries in the woods, reading Braille, and studying music. She also ensured that her students were prepared to enter the classroom with sighted students once they reached high school. Four of her

alums formed a musical group called the Five Blind Boys of Mississippi and eventually found crossover success on the gospel/jubilee hit parade. Helen Keller also visited the school and praised its success.

Martha was recognized for the educational legacy she helped create, winning the Franklin Delano Roosevelt Drama Award in 1942 and the Mississippi Teacher Association Award for Outstanding Teacher of the Year in 1969, the same year she retired.

The Piney Woods School is the largest African American boarding school today, and the second-oldest continuously operating African American boarding school in the United States.

Explore an outdoor environment—a park or any peaceful space you can access—that engages multiple senses for an experimental-learning session of your own. Pay attention to what's around you, and consider the role that the natural world plays in your life.

Tidye Pickett

NOVEMBER 3, 1914–NOVEMBER 17, 1986

In the early 1930s, the only outlets for many young women to hone their sports skills were church leagues and playground pickup games. As a teenager, Tidye Pickett was such a spectacular runner in the Chicago Parks and Playgrounds city championship circuit that coaches began to notice her. By January 1932, she was tying national records for the indoor sixty-yard dash. That winter, she bested two top American runners in the same event. As a result of her unassailable dominance, she and another young Black athlete, Louise Stokes, were invited to join the American 4 × 100 relay team to compete in the 1932 Olympics, held in Los Angeles.

Before the 1928 Olympiad, women were not even allowed to compete in track and field; the myth that jumping and running would compromise women's childbearing organs prevailed. But far more damaging to seventeen-year-old Tidye and Louise was the overt racism they suffered on the team. They had separate and inferior accommodations, and while the rest of the team was honored with a welcome banquet, the two African American athletes had to eat off metal trays in their room, situated near a janitorial station. A teammate—a famous figure in women's track and field and an avowed racist—emptied a pitcher of ice water on the girls while they were asleep in their train bunk.

Worst of all, the duo was replaced in the relay at the last minute by two white athletes. Whether this was a justified substitution remains disputed, but the humiliation was very real. Four years later, Tidye was hesitant to try out for the Berlin Olympics—particularly because that year's host country, Germany, was positioning the Games as a showcase

> "Times were different then. Some people didn't want to admit we were better runners." —T.P.

for Hitler's Aryan supremacy theory. She did make the team and went on to become the first African American woman to compete in the Olympics, but ultimately it was an unfortunate injury, not mistreatment by the Nazis, that ended her Olympic career.

Once her track days were over, Tidye returned to basketball, another sport she had dominated as an adolescent. By 1939, she was headlining a novelty all-Black women's team that came to be known as the Chocolate Co-Eds. Like the Harlem Globetrotters, their act included entertaining side tricks, such as Tidye Pickett running halftime sprints. Indeed, the Co-Eds claimed that they had the "fastest girl runner in the world" on their team.

Another dominant track-and-field athlete at the time was African American Jesse Owens, who was twenty-six when he won four gold medals at the 1936 Olympics. If you could interview Jesse and Tidye about the symbolic impact of their Olympic moments, what would you ask?

Red Wing

FEBRUARY 13, 1884–MARCH 13, 1974

Ho-Chunk (formerly called Winnebago) actress Lillian Margaret St. Cyr, known as Red Wing, was a prolific silent movie actress, appearing in more than seventy short and feature films over a fifteen-year career. Born in Nebraska, orphaned in 1888, and educated at Indian boarding schools, Red Wing married budding Algonquin actor James Young Johnson in 1907. To capitalize on the dime novel and Wild West show fad, the couple reinvented themselves as Princess Red Wing and Young Deer, passing themselves off as "Plains Indians" and reenacting stagecoach battles and the like. Filmmakers in the burgeoning West Coast silent movie industry took notice.

Hollywood did not yet exist, but Red Wing and Young Deer—considered by some to be the first Native American power couple—helped establish it. Red Wing's most famous role was in the 1914 film *The Squaw Man*—legendary director Cecil B. DeMille's debut. In this feature-length film, Red Wing plays a *Madame Butterfly*-esque tragic role: Loved and later abandoned by a white man, she kills herself in despair. It was a major coup for a Native American actress to score a leading role, especially at a time when Indigenous people did not enjoy universal citizenship rights.

> "I was hired mainly because I was a real Indian rather than an actor."
>
> —R.W.

Red Wing starred alongside many of the era's icons in front of the camera and worked as a prop maker, costume designer, and stuntwoman behind the scenes. With the arrival of talkies, she moved to New York City, where she dedicated herself to promoting Native American cultures in a positive light. In addition to designing regalia for tribal members, she took on a variety of clients, including toy shop FAO Schwarz, which asked her to construct costumes for its products.

Throughout the 1920s and '30s, she helped found the American Indian Community House, the leading urban Indigenous center in the tristate area of New York, New Jersey, and Connecticut. Red Wing also became involved with the Indian Unity Alliance, a group advocating for National Indian Day as a federal holiday. Native American Heritage Day, a civil holiday, was finally instated by President George W. Bush in 2008.

Red Wing does not have a star on the Hollywood Walk of Fame, even though Bugs Bunny, Kermit the Frog, Mickey Mouse, Big Bird, and Lassie do. Instead of a sidewalk star, how would you memorialize her, and why? Think big!

Ellen Smith Craft

1826–1891

For enslaved people living in a border state or a coastal city, escape was difficult enough, but flight from the Deep South was rarer still. Ellen Smith Craft not only liberated herself, but she also brought her husband with her.

With very fair skin and European features—her mother was impregnated by a white enslaver—Ellen could pass as white. Despite this relatively privileged appearance, she could not live with her husband, William Craft, because they had different "masters." Deciding to take advantage of Ellen's fair skin, the couple embarked on an audacious escape from rural Georgia in December 1848. She disguised herself as a rich but sickly slave-owning gentleman headed north for treatment; William posed as her dutiful manservant.

Because she was illiterate, Ellen wrapped her arm in a sling to avoid signing hotel and train registries. She also feigned deafness to avoid being pulled into conversation. When someone who knew her in her "former" life as an enslaved woman sat next to her on a train, Ellen held her breath and indicated that light conversational banter was not possible. The subterfuge worked. The couple traveled northward from Savannah to Charleston, Washington, DC, and Baltimore, and arrived in Philadelphia in the free state of Pennsylvania on Christmas Day. They

> "Come, William, it is getting late, so now let us venture upon our perilous journey."
>
> —E.S.C., quoted in *Running a Thousand Miles for Freedom*

had successfully escaped slavery.

Boston, their final destination, embraced them as abolitionist darlings. But Southerners were livid. Not only had Ellen defied race by posing as a white person, but she also defied *gender*, posturing as a man. When the Fugitive Slave Act of 1850 made it a crime to harbor "fugitive slaves," bounty hunters came to Boston to recapture them.

With help from local abolitionist allies, the couple fled for England, where they remained for two decades, raising five children. After living there for ten years, they wrote a book, *Running a Thousand Miles for Freedom; Or, the Escape of William and Ellen Craft from Slavery*.

After Emancipation, the couple returned to the US and opened an agricultural school for the formerly enslaved. Unfortunately, the racism they fled had hardly waned; "night riders" (later known as the Ku Klux Klan) burned down their Savannah plantation, and a second school they opened in Charleston went bankrupt. Although their earthly fortunes were obliterated, the legacy of the Crafts' courage lives on.

Think back to a courageous moment in your life. Imagine you're explaining it to someone younger than you. What was it, why did you do it, and how did you find the courage?

Mabel Ping-Hua Lee

CA. 1896–1966

E arly twentieth-century suffragist marches attracted women by the thousands. One of these—a parade down Manhattan's Fifth Avenue on May 4, 1912—was led by an up-and-coming opinion columnist astride a white horse. She was a sixteen-year-old Chinese immigrant and a Baptist missionary's daughter who believed women's equality was not only a democratic ideal but also an expression of Christian values. Ten thousand women followed her down the parade route.

Mabel Ping-Hua Lee came from a privileged family; her father was among a select category of Chinese men allowed to enter the US under the 1882 Chinese Exclusion Act. As a young girl, she excelled academically at a private missionary academy and earned a competitive scholarship and special visa to study in the United States. This allowed the nine-year-old and her family members to join her father in America. The reunited family settled into a Lower Manhattan tenement apartment in 1905.

By the spring of 1912, Mabel was a high school senior and had become known for the articles she

wrote for the school newspaper, in which she sought to persuade fellow Chinese students to join her in support of women's equality. In her homeland of China, revolutionaries

> ## "The fundamental principle of democracy is equality of opportunity." —M.P.H.L.

had just toppled the Qing dynasty a year before, and she hoped the new government would promote women's rights. As she entered Barnard College that fall, Mabel continued her call for societal advancement for women and girls in America through her writing, with the hope that change would extend to Asia as well.

In 1921, Mabel completed her PhD at Columbia University, becoming the first Chinese woman in the United States to earn a PhD in economics. Her dissertation, *The Economic History of China*, was published as a book. She then traveled to Europe to learn about international economics.

Events both personal and political impeded her dream to start a girls' school in China. Her father passed away in 1924, and she was asked to assume his role as director of the First Chinese Baptist Church of New York City. The unrest of a civil war in China and the 1937 outbreak of the Second Sino-Japanese War also made prolonged visits to China unsafe.

Though Mabel Ping-Hua Lee never resettled in China, she greatly aided New York's Chinatown community by founding the Chinese Christian Center, a hub that provided English lessons, health care services, and kindergarten schooling.

Voting records don't confirm whether Mabel ever voted in the US, nor if she attained citizenship, but her contributions nonetheless helped pave the way for others. What's a sacrifice or hardship you took on so that others could benefit? Why was this action important to you?

Della Irving Hayden

1851–DECEMBER 1924

Because it was illegal to teach slaves to read or write, educational attainment after Emancipation was seen as not only a means of survival but also a sign of virtue and value. The trajectory of Della Irving Hayden's life exemplifies the emergence of the "Negro" civic leader at the turn of the last century.

Reunited with her mother in 1865 after slavery ended and newly able to attend school, Della showed great scholarly potential. In 1872, she started college at the Hampton Normal and Agricultural Institute in Virginia (among her classmates was Booker T. Washington). Part of a wave of higher-education institutions for Black people, the school was founded in 1868 by Black and white missionaries.

Della was affable and spirited but an industrious student as well. She won the first prize for oration at her Hampton commencement with a speech entitled "Our Work as Women." The twenty-dollar prize was presented to her by then First Lady of the United States, Lucy Ware Webb Hayes, who clasped Della's hand in an encouraging shake, telling her, "I hope you may be to your people as your speech said. I trust you will find your work and do it well and may the Lord prosper you." Della said it was the happiest day of her life.

Her 1880 marriage to a fellow Hampton alum lasted only a few months before Della was widowed. She then dedicated the next two decades of her life to her academic career. She became the genteelly named "lady principal" of the

> "My experiences of thirty-three years in the schoolroom have not always been smooth sailing. I cannot save the whole race, but every boy and girl that I can train in the right way will make the race stronger and the state better."
>
> —D.I.H.

Virginia Normal and Collegiate Institute (known today as Virginia State University) in 1890. In 1904, she established the Franklin Normal and Industrial Institute, an agricultural residential college for women. Civically minded, she was also active in the Woman's Christian Temperance Union, the Young Women's Christian Association, and church committees in her small town of Franklin, Virginia.

In 1924, the town's first fatal vehicular accident claimed Della Irving Hayden's life. Her lifelong generosity and desire to uplift her people are celebrated in Virginia's Western Tidewater region and honored by the Franklin, Virginia, high school that bears her name.

What's a skill that you excel at?
Teach a friend or family member how to do it,
and reflect on what the process of sharing
your gifts teaches you about yourself.

Sono Osato

AUGUST 29, 1919–DECEMBER 26, 2018

The life of Sono Osato is a compelling reflection of the twentieth-century Japanese American experience, with some groundbreaking leaps and turns. Born to a Japanese father and a mother of French Canadian descent, Sono first fell in love with ballet in Monaco on an extended European trip with her culture-loving mother. Sono started private lessons once the family returned to Chicago, and she soon displayed prodigious talent. She was invited to join Col. Wassily de Basil's Ballets Russes—the most famous ballet company in the world—at the age of fourteen, making her the youngest dancer, first American, and first ballerina of Japanese descent to join the storied troupe. After six years of touring with the company, she returned to the US to study at the School of American Ballet in New York City and joined American Ballet Theater (ABT) in 1941.

Sono was proud of her Japanese heritage (while touring in Europe, she refused the suggestion to change her name to something that sounded more Russian), but she faced profound xenophobia in America. Because of her ancestry, the US government forbade her to travel with ABT to Mexico and California when the company went on tour. After World War II began and her father was sent to an internment camp, Sono, like tens of thousands of other nisei (second-generation Japanese Americans), felt pressured to adopt her mother's surname, Fitzpatrick.

> "I could never have been accepted as Ivy Smith in films, or later, on television. Only the power of illusion created between performers and audiences across the footlights can transcend political preference, moral attitudes, and racial prejudice." —S.O.

During wartime, Sono became part of New York's intellectual, antifascist arts scene. Because of her dance pedigree, she scored the role of a lifetime: playing Ivy Smith (Miss Turnstiles) in the original 1944 production of *On the Town*. Given the racial tenor of the time and the risk-averse mentality of the commercial Broadway theater world, casting Sono as the "all-American girl" lead was an audacious move. But *On the Town* was composed and choreographed by legendary duo Leonard Bernstein and Jerome Robbins, whose worldview as cosmopolitan, gay Jewish intellectuals compelled them to take risks. Sono remained with the cast long enough for her father to be released from internment and finally see her perform. The show was a sensation and remains a perennial favorite in the theater repertoire.

Sono also appeared in several motion pictures, including a role alongside Frank Sinatra in a 1948 musical called *The Kissing Bandit*, in which she played a Mexican temptress who does a wild dance with a whip. Later in her career, she focused on assisting dancers through the Sono Osato Scholarship Program for Graduate Studies, which she founded in 2006.

It's been said that until Sono's performance in *On the Town*, no Asian woman had been featured on the Great White Way since Anna May Wong (see page 28) in 1930. Is there a play or musical that you especially admire? What about it stands out to you?

Mary McLeod Bethune

JULY 10, 1875–MAY 18, 1955

fter the Civil War ended, many newly freed people sought to further their education, as it had previously been unlawful for enslaved people to learn to read. The fifteenth child of former slaves, Mary McLeod Bethune not only learned to read and write, but she also became a champion for education and a civic leader who advised no fewer than four US presidents (Coolidge, Hoover, Roosevelt, and Truman).

Social clubs were a primary vehicle for Black Americans to establish civic and social standing while doing good works that uplifted the less fortunate. Three of the most long-standing of these clubs—the NAACP, the National Council of Negro Women, and the United Negro College Fund—all have Mary to thank for their establishment. With her suffragist friends, she advocated for the 1920 passage of the Nineteenth

MARY McLEOD BETHUNE
1875–1955
Let her works praise her

Amendment, giving women the right to vote. (Sadly, extreme voter suppression persisted for people of color—the Voting Rights Act of 1965 didn't become law until ten years after Mary's death.)

Fellow suffragist and First Lady Eleanor Roosevelt advocated for Mary to have a role in her husband's administration. President Franklin D. Roosevelt named Mary director of Negro Affairs of the National Youth Administration in 1936, making her the highest-ranking Black woman in government and the de facto leader of FDR's unofficial "Black Cabinet." In 1945, she was one of the few women of color among the more than 3,500 delegates and advisers from fifty nations sent to the founding conference of the United Nations.

Mary was also a trailblazer in education. Back in 1904, while residing in Daytona Beach, Florida, she wished to open a boarding school for local African American girls. Undaunted by the challenge of raising money to found a school, she appealed to the community by selling desserts and homemade pastries. In 1923, the school merged with the all-men Cookman Institute to become Bethune-Cookman University, one of now 107 historically Black colleges and universities (HBCUs) in the US.

_____

"Next to God we are indebted to women, first for life itself, and then for making it worth having."

—M.M.B.

_____

A stateswoman, philanthropist, and humanitarian, Mary McLeod Bethune is one of the most celebrated women in US history. A statue was erected in her honor in Washington, DC, in 1974, and her portrait appeared on a 1985 memorial postage stamp.

Mary's most far-out accolade is probably the Venusian crater named for her in 1991. Celebrate her by going stargazing on a clear night. While you're out there, invent your own foremother-inspired constellation!

Augusta Savage

FEBRUARY 29, 1892–MARCH 27, 1962

B orn on a leap day, Augusta Savage was perhaps destined to sculpt her life on her own terms. As a child, she would abandon herself to her creative mind, forming small animals and other playthings out of the firm red soil around her Florida home. Despite her pious father's disapproval of such "graven images"—Augusta said he nearly "whipped all the art out of me"—she showed talent, winning a prize for the most original exhibit at the 1919 West Palm Beach County Fair. Encouraged by this award, she made her way to New York, cradle of the Harlem Renaissance.

Although she was a young widow with a small child in tow, Augusta was determined to go to art school. She earned a coveted and competitive slot at the Cooper Union, where she finished her four-year art school course in three years and received commissions to sculpt famous African American leaders such as W. E. B. Du Bois and Marcus Garvey. In 1921, she was awarded a prestigious spot in the Fontainebleau School of Fine Arts summer program in France. Sadly, when the committee discovered she was African American, they rescinded the invitation. Though outraged, she soldiered on, juggling odd jobs to support herself, her child, her now paralyzed father, and other family members who had migrated to New York after a hurricane destroyed their Florida home.

She eventually made it to Paris in 1929 on a fellowship that allowed her to travel and exhibit her work throughout Europe, including at the

Salon d'Automne and the Grand Palais in Paris. She returned to New York in 1932 and established the Savage Studio of Arts and Crafts in Harlem, where young students like painter Jacob Lawrence got their start before becoming art-world stars.

The first African American elected to the National Association of Women Painters and Sculptors, Augusta also created the Harlem Community Art Center under the federal Works Progress Administration (WPA) program in 1936. First Lady Eleanor Roosevelt used it as a model for other community art centers around the country.

Augusta's realistic sculptures of African Americans harbored a sense of the subjects' souls. She was one of four women and the only African American to be commissioned for the 1939 New York World's Fair. Her sculpture *Lift Every Voice and Sing*, named after the hymn by

> "I have created nothing really beautiful, really lasting, but if I can inspire one of these youngsters to develop the talent I know they possess, then my monument will be in their work." —A.S.

James Weldon Johnson and John Rosamond Johnson that is the Black national anthem, was one of the most photographed pieces at the fair. Also known as *The Harp*, this sixteen-foot-tall work displayed a dozen singing Black youths, each representing a string of the harp. Unable to afford bronze or stone, Augusta sculpted plaster, which she painted black to resemble basalt. At the close of the fair, the works, deemed temporary, were demolished. The sculpture exists only in photographic format today.

After several commercial disappointments, Augusta retreated to an artists' community in Upstate New York in 1945, devoting herself to teaching art to local children. Is there someone in history or your family who you believe never got the appreciation they deserved? How would you celebrate them today?

Xue Jinqin

1883–1960

In the suffragist 1920s, support for gender equality was germinating in progressive circles in China. Few, however, imagined that one of the most inspiring feminist speeches would be delivered by a nineteen-year-old Chinese exchange student in progressive San Francisco. Her name was Xue Jinqin.

When studying in Shanghai, Jinqin had already gained the nickname "China's Joan of Arc" for a speech she gave in 1901 in which she spoke out against Chinese concessions to foreign powers. As the Qing dynasty declined, advocates of the Chinese reform movement, including Jinqin, pushed for a stronger, more modern China.

In 1902, Jinqin enrolled at the University of California, Berkeley, seeking to benefit from the American educational system and bring modern ideas back to China. She was immediately embraced by progressive groups, such as the ladies' chapter of the Chinese Empire Reform Association, in San Francisco's booming Chinatown. Because of her oratory fame, she was invited to deliver a speech in San Francisco about her perceptions of the United States and her homeland. A local newspaper, *Chung Sai Yat Po*, published an article praising her speech, which was delivered in Chinese to an audience of about a thousand. Unfortunately, there is no recording of the speech, but the article describes her main points:

- The cultural practice of foot binding causes pain, reduces mobility, and is demoralizing; it must end.

- A nation cannot thrive if half its population is restrained.

- Women's schools are necessary nationwide "so that all twenty million women in China can acquire reasoning and practice professions,

> "Men and women are equal and should enjoy the privileges of equals." —X.J.

thus allowing them to move forward on a complementary footing with men."

- Chinese women would benefit from emulating modern Western lifestyles, including gaining more education. Educated women, she said, would make better mothers and stronger workers, and this would help build a modern China.

Xue Jinqin insisted that these were not only moral imperatives, but they also made economic sense—a position that still holds resonance today.

In a 1903 speech, Jinqin said, "China doesn't need missionaries, but she needs teachers of commerce, of industry, of liberal thought." Write a short public message stating the top three things you think your country needs right now.

Sonia Sotomayor

JUNE 25, 1954–

Sonia Sotomayor was born to Puerto Rican parents Celina Baez, a World War II Women's Army Auxiliary Corps member, and Juan Sotomayor, a factory laborer with a third-grade education. The family won a lottery to live in one of the public housing projects in the Bronx, but misfortune befell them: Sonia's father died when she was just nine years old, and her mother had to work six days a week to support her and her brother.

Watching reruns of the 1950s and '60s hit TV drama *Perry Mason*, Sonia grew enthralled with the law. After graduating at the top of her class at Cardinal Spellman High School in 1972, she won a full scholarship to Princeton University and graduated with her BA in 1976. Next was Yale Law School, where she also excelled.

Fresh out of law school in 1979, she prosecuted grim criminal cases as a Manhattan assistant district attorney. She then pivoted to a private commercial law practice and gained seats on state boards pertaining to issues facing low-income communities and people with HIV/AIDS. Knowing that transparency and justice in campaign finance have

enormous impacts on laws and policy, Sonia enthusiastically accepted an appointment as a judge for the US District Court for the Southern District of New York in 1992, becoming the court's youngest judge to date. A lifelong Yankees fan, she became

> "I decided that if I were going to make use of my role as a Supreme Court justice, it would be to inspire people to realize that, first, I was just like them and second, if I could do it, so could they." —S.S.

the celebrated "judge who saved baseball" in arguably her most famous case, 1995's *Silverman v. Major League Baseball Player Relations Committee, Inc.* The preliminary injunction she delivered ended the Major League Baseball stalemate, one of the longest work stoppages in the history of professional sports.

In 1997, Sonia was appointed to the US Court of Appeals for the Second Circuit by President Bill Clinton.

As the first Latina judge on the court, she presided over more than three thousand appeals and wrote approximately 380 opinions. After her time on the Court of Appeals, she was named the first Latina US Supreme Court justice in 2009. In this position, Sonia has championed liberal causes such as reproductive rights and prison reform. As a beneficiary of affirmative action for her undergraduate admission to the Ivy League, she is a steadfast advocate for jurisprudence that provides students from underserved and humble origins with fair access to education.

Eleven years after her appointment to the Supreme Court, Sonia Sotomayor's delivery of the oath of office to Kamala Harris, the first Black, South Asian, and woman vice president, proved a powerful symbolic moment.

Justice Sotomayor went from being a latchkey kid to the third woman appointed to the US Supreme Court (Sandra Day O'Connor and Ruth Bader Ginsburg were the first two). When you were a kid, what did you dream of being when you grew up? What parts of that vision remain with you today?

Katherine Johnson

AUGUST 26, 1918–FEBRUARY 24, 2020

I t's hard to imagine a time when computations were done either by enormous machines the size of a multicar garage or by supersmart humans who ran complex mathematical sequences the old-fashioned way, with slide rules, pencils, chalkboards, and their brains. Katherine Johnson, who worked at NASA from 1953 until 1986, was one of the latter—astronaut John Glenn said he trusted her calculations more than those of any machine.

As an adolescent, Katherine loved math, but the schools for African American children in White Sulphur Springs, West Virginia, only went up to sixth grade. To support Katherine's studies, her family moved to the nearby town of Institute, where Katherine finished high school at age fourteen. Because the high school was located on the campus of West Virginia State University, it was an easy transition for Katherine to matriculate at the historically Black college. She was so advanced in math that her mentor, William W. Schieffelin Claytor (the third African American to earn a mathematics doctorate from an American university), had to create a customized curriculum for her.

In 1937, at the age of eighteen, Katherine graduated summa cum laude, with degrees in mathematics and French. Two years later, she was selected as one of three African American students and the only woman to attend graduate school at West Virginia University. Soon after enrolling, however, she left the program for marriage and motherhood.

Fast-forward to June 1941: As part of the war effort to galvanize as much of the populace as possible, President Franklin D. Roosevelt signed Executive Order 8802, barring racial discrimination in the defense industry. By 1943, the Langley Memorial Aeronautical Laboratory—as NASA was then known—began advertising jobs for Black women mathematicians.

Katherine was one of these hires at Langley, where her geometry acumen allowed her to calculate spacecraft trajectories and windows for launches, returns, and emergency landings. Her superior computational skills contributed to several historic orbital missions, culminating with the Apollo moon landing in 1969 and the genesis of the Space Shuttle program in the early 1980s.

After she "retired" in 1986, she published more than two dozen technical papers and groundbreaking reports. In addition to being presented the 2015 Presidential Medal of Freedom by President Obama at age ninety-seven, she was bestowed the

honor of having a NASA building named after her: the Katherine G. Johnson Computational Research Facility in Hampton, Virginia.

> "I counted everything. I counted the steps to the road, the steps up to church, the number of dishes and silverware I washed . . . anything that could be counted, I did." —K.J.

In the 2016 film *Hidden Figures*, Katherine was portrayed by Taraji P. Henson, who memorably stood in front of chalkboards filled with complex formulas. What's the most complicated thing you know by heart? It could be a recipe, a song, or indeed a computation!

Komako Kimura

1887–1980

O n October 27, 1917, a parade of women took to New York City's Fifth Avenue to demand the right to vote. Among the twenty thousand protesters was Komako Kimura, a Japanese feminist and entertainer who waved both an American and a Japanese flag. She was visiting the US to learn about suffragism, a concept for which the Japanese language didn't have an equivalent word.

Komako, who had been a stage actress since age four, refused to abide by the Confucian patriarchy. To avoid being forced into an arranged marriage, she ran away at age fourteen and threw herself into dance and kabuki theater. While studying at the Imperial Actresses Training School, Komako experienced an unplanned pregnancy. Somehow she managed to hide her condition, but once the school officials learned she had birthed a child out of wedlock, they expelled her. Nevertheless, she performed in more than five hundred plays over her career, even appearing in Shakespearean roles. (Though women thespians did exist in Japan at the time, it was still controversial for women to perform Shakespeare.) Theater was liberating, she said, because on stage, women could speak to men on equal footing.

In 1912, at age twenty-five, Komako cofounded the True New Women's Association, one of a few burgeoning feminist organizations of the time. This group sponsored a lecture series and published a magazine, *The New True Women*, in which Komako criticized traditional Japanese society's subjugation of women, including high-maintenance hairstyles and clothing that restricted movement. Further, the publication's manifesto contended that marriage contracts were no more than a form of bondage. Komako and her editorial colleagues also advocated for birth control, a truly radical idea for this era in Japan.

Komako's second husband, who was modern and progressive in his stances, joined her on the 1917 voyage to New York. They returned to Japan in 1918, but by then the Japanese government had come to consider the couple's work dangerous. Officials shut down the magazine and banned Komako from participating in public gatherings, such as theater. Not surprisingly, she resisted by offering free admission to plays she staged in the two theaters she ran. Komako was then arrested for flouting the authorities. She served as her own defense lawyer, gained more publicity and support for her feminist cause, and was eventually acquitted.

After the trial, the couple moved back to the United States. When they returned to Japan in 1925, Komako Kimura focused on the arts and other pursuits. She lived to see Japanese women finally win the right to vote in 1945.

> "Sisters of the world, let's gather our power, and shock the men who belittle us by saying, 'What can women do?'" —K.K.

Who is an entertainer or artist you admire for their outspoken stances? Draw them leading a protest. What is the cause? What does their sign say?

Mary Kaye

JANUARY 9, 1924–FEBRUARY 17, 2007

If you're familiar with electric guitars, you may have heard of the legendary Fender Stratocaster model, played by a veritable who's who of old-school rock 'n' roll—a boys' club spanning Buddy Holly to Eric Clapton, George Harrison to Jimi Hendrix. But did you know that the earliest custom-made Strat was a translucent white-and-gold masterpiece, coveted by collectors and named after a woman of Hawaiian descent? That same woman invented the term "lounge music" and became known as the "First Lady of Rock and Roll" for her vigorous and swinging playing style. Her name was Mary Kaye.

Born under the name Malia Ka'aihue, Mary started performing with her father at age nine and soon went from playing with a ukulele-centered Hawaiian act to leading her own musical group. Adopting a more Anglicized first name, she called it the Mary Ka'aihue Trio. Later dubbed the Mary Kaye Trio, the band was all about upbeat jazz covers, chirpy calypso ditties, killer swing riffs—and great comedic timing.

Though steadily gigging, they were far from megastars. In fact, one night in the early 1950s, the trio found that they were double-booked with another act at the Last Frontier, a Las Vegas hotel with live entertainment. The headliner had no intention of budging from the main stage. "I suggested a stage be built in the bar area, and it could be called a 'lounge,'" said Mary. The manager took her suggestion, and the rest is Vegas history. The wild after-hours atmosphere soon attracted none other than Frank Sinatra and the Rat Pack: Over the first week of the show, the high-rollin' squad dropped $120,000 on gambling, drinking, and partying until the wee hours. The Vegas Strip—today an iconic playground of venues and hotels for celebrities, hopefuls, and hangers-on—was born.

To compete with all the carousing, acts had to sing loud, play big, and ham it up. Mary's swingin', singer-based act was a hit with celebrities like Marlene Dietrich, Sammy Davis Jr., Dean Martin, and Elvis, who once complimented Mary's guitar chops. Even though she posed with the custom Stratocaster in a 1956 publicity photo, she in fact played a different make called a D'Angelico.

The trio made movies and albums, surviving on the Strip until the mid-'60s, when Beatlemania ushered in a new musical taste. Mary Kaye continued to play solo into the 1970s, and in 2003, Fender gifted her a customized guitar.

Write down your dream musical act: the venue, the staging and clothing, the songs, the instruments . . .

NIGHT IN VEGAS

Josephine St. Pierre Ruffin

AUGUST 31, 1842–MARCH 13, 1924

Josephine St. Pierre grew up in Boston's Beacon Hill neighborhood, an elite African American enclave. She married prominent Bostonian George Lewis Ruffin at age fifteen and devoted herself to family and civic life. When the Civil War began, she served as a volunteer recruiter for Black Union Army conscripts. She also supported the Kansas Freedmen's Relief Association by collecting money and mutual aid for Exodusters, freed slaves migrating from the Deep South to Kansas.

Josephine's upper-middle-class background and elite bearing afforded her privilege and access to Boston's white society as well. She

joined the New England Woman's Press Association and, in 1869, cofounded Boston's American Woman Suffrage Association with suffragists and abolitionists Lucy Stone and Julia Ward Howe. Josephine was also good friends with Susan B. Anthony, Elizabeth Cady Stanton, and Booker T. Washington.

Widowed in 1886, Josephine continued to pursue her interests in women's welfare; the educational, social, and moral uplift of African Americans; and women's civic duty. She combined these topics in her 1890 launch of the *Woman's Era*, the first national newspaper published by and for African American women. As the

Black clubwomen's movement grew in popularity, the *Woman's Era* became a standard-bearer for educated, upper-middle-class Black women nationwide. During its seven years of publication, the paper covered social events; provided health and beauty tips; and presented important political and civic commentary regarding elections, discrimination, and the rise of domestic terrorism in the South.

In alignment with the ideals of the publication, Josephine cofounded Boston's Woman's Era Club, an advocacy group that helped organize the first National Conference of Colored Women of America in 1895. Some of the summit's attendees came together to form what became

> "If laws are unjust, they must be continually broken until they are altered." —J.S.R.

the National Association of Colored Women's Clubs, of which Mary Church Terrell (see page 172) was president.

Josephine St. Pierre Ruffin believed that gender equality would open the door to racial equality. Over the course of the twentieth century, social and political activism became more deliberate, but her early contributions to the advancement of African American women are undeniable.

Imagine that the *Woman's Era* is still in print today. Pitch an article for an upcoming issue. Here are some feature titles from the newspaper's past to get you started:

The Problem of the Unemployed

"Difficulties"* of Colonization

Women at Home

Music and Drama

Women in Business

Club Gossip

*Quotes added.

Elizabeth Key Grinstead

1630–JANUARY 20, 1665

Understanding the paradox of Elizabeth Key Grinstead's astonishing seventeenth-century lawsuit requires unpacking the twisted logic of enslavement and the irrational mathematics of racial purity.

Elizabeth was the illegitimate daughter of Thomas Key, a white landowner who decided to return to England. He sent the six-year-old girl to live with a wealthy tobacco planter as an indentured servant, extracting a promise that she be treated like a member of the family and manumitted at age fifteen. But Key died, and the farmer sold Elizabeth to someone new, who moved his farm and human "property" to a more rural part of Virginia.

One of the farmer's white indentured servants, a Brit named William Grinstead, had sold himself into indenture in the hopes of making a fortune in the New World. Elizabeth, now twenty years old, and William fell in love and had a son. By this time, William's servitude had ended, and he began training to be a lawyer. But because of her maternal heritage, Elizabeth was not manumitted.

> "We conceive the said Elizabeth ought to be free and that her last Master should give her Corn and Clothes and give her satisfaction for the time she hath served longer than She ought to have done."
>
> —Court ruling

Indeed, when the new owner died in 1655, his heirs reclassified Elizabeth as a "Negro" and property of the estate.

Elizabeth sued for her freedom, with her common-law husband serving as her counsel. Their argument: Because her white father was a free man Elizabeth should also be free. After appeals and overturns, she won unequivocal freedom on July 21, 1656. She and William wed and had another child.

But the precedent of losing "property" was unbearable to Virginia slaveholders. In 1662, the Virginia Colony passed a law stating that slavery was hereditary, a condition for life, and that, unlike in England, a child's freedom was based on the mother's status, not the father's. For the next two centuries, white slave owners were able to renounce any children they fathered as a result of sexually assaulting enslaved women. While Elizabeth Key Grinstead's case was in many ways a Pyrrhic victory, it is still

remarkable that for a short moment in the colonial era a Black woman had the law on her side. This part of the story would inspire generations to come.

Has a seemingly good idea ever backfired on you? If you could go back in time, how would you rewrite the outcome?

Lorraine Hansberry

MAY 19, 1930–JANUARY 12, 1965

Before she made history as Broadway's first Black woman playwright, Lorraine Hansberry grew up in a whites-only neighborhood in Chicago. Her parents, longtime contributors to the NAACP, withstood physical attacks and demands for them to move—until a court ordered them to do so. The Hansberrys took the appeal to the US Supreme Court, where their right to buy the home was ultimately upheld. The decision to overturn the eviction was due to a technicality rather than racial redress, but it still set a precedent for Black families fighting restrictive homeownership regulations.

At the University of Wisconsin—Madison, Lorraine fought for civil rights and social integration, joining the Communist Party USA and helping integrate a dormitory. After two years of collegiate life, she decamped to New York City, where she wrote for Paul Robeson's progressive Black newspaper and later for the Daughters of Bilitis, the nation's first lesbian political rights organization. Lorraine met Jewish writer Robert Nemiroff at a political rally; though she identified as a lesbian, they wed in June 1953.

Inspired by Lorraine's childhood community, the story of a loving Black American family struggling to make their way in the face of discrimination later became the theme of her groundbreaking 1959 play, *A Raisin in the Sun*. It was a smash Broadway hit, running for 530 shows and making twenty-nine-year-old Lorraine the first Black woman playwright and the youngest American to win a New York Drama

> "As of today, if I am asked abroad if I am a free citizen of the United States of America, I must only say what is true: *No.*" —L.H.

Critics Circle Award. Two years later, iconic actor Sidney Poitier headlined the film version.

Lorraine's political fervor gained intensity as the civil rights movement accelerated. At a momentous 1964 New York town hall forum organized by a coalition of Black activists and entertainers, including Sidney Poitier, James Baldwin, and Ruby Dee, Lorraine challenged white liberals to take responsibility: "We have to find some way with these dialogues to . . . encourage the white liberal to stop being a liberal and become an American radical."

Unfortunately, Lorraine Hansberry did not live to see the societal changes of the late 1960s and '70s; she succumbed to pancreatic cancer in 1965 at age thirty-four. *A Raisin in the Sun* remains one of the most performed plays in American theater.

Write the synopsis of a play featuring a family or group of people you find interesting and inspiring. Why did you choose them? What struggle do they face, and how do they triumph?

Zitkála-Šá

FEBRUARY 22, 1876–JANUARY 26, 1938

Zitkála-Šá, a member of the Yankton Dakota tribe, was eight years old when she first experienced involuntary assimilation: She was carried off from her South Dakota reservation to boarding school in Indiana and forced to cut her hair. Her Native moccasins, clothing, and cultural traditions were exchanged for a stiff uniform, Quaker prayers, and a Christian name: Gertrude Simmons. The alienation and estrangement she felt on her home reservation upon her return to South Dakota led her to adopt an entirely new name: Zitkála-Šá (which translates to Red Bird).

She studied violin at the New England Conservatory of Music, but financial and health issues derailed the completion of her college degree. Zitkála-Šá performed at the 1900 Paris Exposition and later made history by writing the libretto and songs for *The Sun Dance*, the first opera written by a Native American.

"I was not wholly conscious of myself, but was more keenly alive to the fire within. It was as if I were the activity, and my hands and feet were only experiments for my spirit to work upon." —Z.-Š.

The opera was based on a federally banned sacred Dakota ritual and premiered in Utah in 1913.

Angered by the poverty and deprivation faced by the Yankton Dakota tribe juxtaposed with the relative opulence enjoyed by the Anglo colonizers, Zitkála-Šá used journalism as a form of dissent, writing articles for *The Atlantic* and *Harper's* that decried the degradation of Indigenous lifeways and the erasure of their cultures. These exposés cost Zitkála-Šá her job as a music teacher at Pennsylvania's elite Carlisle Indian School, but they also introduced her to a new mission: storytelling and culture-keeping. Her book of oral histories, *Old Indian Legends*, was published in 1901, followed by a *Harper's* article ("Why I Am a Pagan") reinforcing Indigenous spirituality in 1902 and *American Indian Stories*, a collection of childhood allegories and fiction, in 1921.

Zitkála-Šá married Captain Raymond Talefase Bonnin in 1902, and the pair moved to the Uintah and Ouray Reservation in Utah. Joining the Society of American Indians, she became a vocal critic of the US federal government's American Indian policy. She later lived in Washington, DC, and edited the society's *American Indian Magazine* but frequently traveled across the country to deliver speeches on Indigenous rights. Many attribute the 1924 Indian Citizenship Act, which granted US citizenship to Indigenous people, to her advocacy.

In 1926, the couple founded the National Council of American Indians to unite tribes across the country in the fight for suffrage, which was missing from the Citizenship Act. Voting rights and expanded tribal self-determination were eventually won in 1934 with the passage of the Indian Reorganization Act.

What is the story behind your first name?
Do you identify with it?

Pauli Murray

NOVEMBER 20, 1910–JULY 1, 1985

Pauli Murray was a lawyer and legal scholar; womanist poet and author; human, civil, and labor rights activist; Episcopal priest; LGBTQIA+ pioneer; and friend to everyone from W. E. B. Du Bois and Langston Hughes to Eleanor Roosevelt. Pauli's childhood was marked by trauma: Agnes, Pauli's mother, died in 1914, and three years later, William Murray, Pauli's father, was suffering from typhoid and was consigned to a mental institution. Living with relatives in North Carolina, Pauli found refuge in books and graduated at the top of their high school class in 1926, at age fifteen.

In their first encounter with what Pauli would later call "Jane Crow," the young graduate learned that their preferred college, Columbia University, did not accept women. This was the first of several academic disappointments; Pauli was later rejected from the University of North Carolina School of Law due to racial segregation. At Howard Law School, where they enrolled as the only woman in 1939, Pauli was overtly mocked by male classmates, even though Pauli's legal arguments predicted the demise of *Plessy v. Ferguson*, the very law that established Jim Crow. Pauli went on to graduate first in their Howard class and was awarded the Rosenwald Fellowship, which many previous valedictorians used to attend Harvard University. But Pauli was again denied because they were a woman.

Also unconventional for the time were Pauli's political affiliations, which included the leftist Workers Defense League—an organization that supported the young activist after a 1940 arrest for refusing to leave the whites-only section of a Virginia bus—and the Communist Party, an alliance that got Pauli in trouble during the McCarthy Red Scare of the 1950s.

"I've lived to see my lost causes found." —P.M.

Pauli's distinguished career had several pivots: In 1945, they became California's first African American deputy attorney general, a position in which the lawyer helped influence landmark legislation against segregated juries and fought for equal rights for women. The legal tome Pauli compiled was dubbed "the bible for civil rights lawyers" by Thurgood Marshall. Creatively minded, Pauli also wrote many volumes of poetry.

After teaching law at the University of Ghana in 1960, Pauli became the first African American to earn a JSD degree from Yale Law School, in 1965. The following year, they cofounded the National Organization for Women. And in 1977, Pauli Murray made history once more as the first African American woman to be ordained a priest in the Episcopal Church—the same entity that would name Pauli a saint in 2012, twenty-seven years after their passing.

It is a bitter irony that Pauli was denied opportunities because of their gender, given that they expressed gender fluidity over the years. What books, movies, or other cultural markers of today do you think Pauli would have appreciated had they existed in the mid-twentieth century?

Grace Lee Boggs

JUNE 27, 1915–OCTOBER 5, 2015

Born to immigrant parents (an entrepreneurial father who ran a Chinese restaurant and a mother who modeled feminist grit and conviction), Grace Lee Boggs was granted a scholarship to Barnard College at age sixteen. She earned her BA in 1935 and a PhD in philosophy from Bryn Mawr College five years later. Unable to find work in academia due to anti-Chinese racism, Grace took a low-paying clerical job at a library in Chicago. All she could afford on her ten-dollar weekly salary was a squalid basement apartment. The conditions were so deplorable that she joined local housing protests—thus igniting her involvement in far-left politics. Her philosophical ruminations over Marx and Hegel quickly paled in interest as she took up the fight for tenants' rights alongside her Black neighbors.

In 1953, she moved to Detroit and reconnected with an African American autoworker named James Boggs, whom she had met years earlier. They shared such compatibility on their first date that they decided to get married. Among Detroit's most legendary labor and civil rights activists, the pair went on to champion a plethora of causes, from feminism and environmentalism to Black Power and Asian American rights. Anticapitalism was the backbone of their doctrine, but over the years, Grace's tactics shifted from revolutionary uprising to grassroots self-determination. Her work with community organizations, food co-ops, and urban gardens was as

> "History is not the past. It is the stories we tell about the past. *How* we tell these stories—triumphantly or self-critically, metaphysically or dialectically—has a lot to do with whether we cut short or advance our evolution as human beings."
>
> —G.L.B.

prominent in her activism as giving lectures and writing books.

Grace Lee Boggs's political evolution from Trotskyism to community empowerment was paralleled in her ideological shift from Malcolm X's Black Power doctrine to the nonviolence tactics of Martin Luther King Jr. Over the course of her life, she became increasingly convinced that good neighbors and local pride were powerful antidotes to blight and crime. Programs such as Detroit Summer, which she cofounded in 1992, bring volunteers from across the nation to build community gardens, paint murals, repair homes, and organize musical events—this model of community-engaged activism has been replicated around the world.

Follow in Grace's footsteps and cultivate your green thumb by spending an afternoon at a community garden or simply tending a plant on your windowsill.

Queen Emma

JANUARY 2, 1836–APRIL 25, 1885

I n keeping with the traditional Hawaiian custom of hānai, Emma Kalanikaumaka'amano Kaleleonālani Na'ea Rooke was adopted by her childless maternal aunt and given an upper-class education at the Royal School. Among her seven classmates at the elite missionary school was her future husband, Prince Alexander Liholiho (the future King Kamehameha IV). Though their June 1856 wedding was feted with national fanfare, some disputed her lineage because her maternal grandfather was part British. In a land of complex lineages and disputed successions, this was not her last political heartache.

The royal couple busied themselves with raising money for an Anglican cathedral in Honolulu, and in 1858, they welcomed a son, Albert Edward Kauikeaouli Leiopapa a Kamehameha. England's Queen Victoria, pleased with the couple's efforts to promote the Anglican Church in Hawai'i, agreed to be the child's godmother by proxy. Tragically, Albert died at age four, likely of appendicitis, in 1862; King Kamehameha IV passed away a year later.

Despite these tragedies in her personal life, the dowager queen turned her grief into a drive to help her people. She established the Queen's Hospital, which still provides free health care for people of Native Hawaiian ancestry to this day, and she founded private Episcopal schools for both boys and girls, even providing the tuition for Native Hawaiian girls to attend the finishing school.

In 1865 and 1866, Queen Emma traveled to Europe and the United States, finally meeting her longtime epistolary friend Queen Victoria as well as Napoleon III and Grand Duke Frederick II, and attending a state dinner hosted by President Andrew Johnson. Despite a distance of over 7,200 miles, she maintained a devoted correspondence with Queen Victoria for the rest of her life.

Queen Emma's second political disappointment occurred in 1874, as a result of the death of Hawai'i's

> "We have yet the right to dispose of our country as we wish, and be assured that it will never be to a Republic!" —E.K.K.N.R.

sixth monarch, King Lunalilo. As the widow of a prior monarch, Emma was the popular choice to succeed the king; furthermore, her pro-British, anti-American stance pleased many who feared American imperialism. However, the legislative assembly selected David Kalākaua as Lunalilo's successor. After King David's untimely demise, his sister, Queen Lili'uokalani (see page 42), became the first and only queen regnant of Hawai'i and the kingdom's final monarch.

(see page 42)

In the United States, November 28 is now recognized as an Episcopalian holiday: the feast of Queen Emma and King Kamehameha IV.

Queen Emma was baptized as an Anglican under the name Emma Alexandrina Francis Agnes Lowder Byde Rooke Young Kaleleokalani. What would your honorific title be? Draw and decorate a crest using at least six names.

Cicely Tyson

DECEMBER 19, 1924–JANUARY 28, 2021

The daughter of working-class Caribbean immigrants, Cicely Tyson felt destined for greatness. As a secretary at the Red Cross, she proclaimed to her coworkers: "God did not put me on the face of this earth to bang on a typewriter for the rest of my life!"

Cicely was in her thirties when she was discovered as a model and then by a film casting agent. Her conservative, religious mother kicked her out of the house but eventually let her know how proud she was of her achievements. When Cicely became the first Black American woman to win an Academy Honorary Award, in 2018 at age ninety-three, she lifted her statue aloft. "Mom, I know you didn't want me to do this," she chuckled, "but I did—and here it is!"

Aware of the entertainment industry's outsized influence on the human psyche, Cicely refused movie and theater roles that demeaned Black Americans. Her defiance cost her a lot of work over the years, but casting agents be damned. Since its beginnings, Hollywood had anointed only a few Black actors—typically with fair skin and straightened hair—with celebrity status. Regal and statuesque in African attire and natural hairdos, Cicely was a symbol of the cultural shift in beauty standards during the 1960s and '70s. She gave groundbreaking performances in movies ranging from 1972's *Sounder*, for which she was nominated for the Academy Award for Best Actress, to 1991's *Fried Green Tomatoes* and 2011's *The Help*. At the age of eighty-eight, her performance in Broadway's 2013 revival of *The Trip to Bountiful* won her a Tony Award, making her theater's oldest honoree at the time.

Cicely's television roles, such as Kunta Kinte's mother in the history-making 1977 miniseries *Roots* (in which

> "I saw that I could not afford the luxury of just being an actress. So I made a choice to use my career as a platform to address the issues of the race I was born into." —C.T.

Maya Angelou played her mother) and the title character in 1974's *The Autobiography of Miss Jane Pittman*, were portrayals of Black women with psychological depth and tenacity that audiences had never seen before. To inform her role as Jane, a 110-year-old Southerner whose culminating moment is taking a sip of water from a whites-only drinking fountain, Cicely visited nursing homes and studied the movements of older people.

In the 1980s, Cicely and jazz legend Miles Davis (her on-and-off partner for more than two decades) were America's Black "it couple." Beyond the red carpet, she was a committed humanitarian, founding the Dance Theatre of Harlem after Martin Luther King Jr.'s 1968 assassination and serving as a UNICEF goodwill ambassador.

As she herself advanced in years, Cicely Tyson remained stately and spry, receiving a Presidential Medal of Freedom in 2016 and even promoting her second memoir, which was released just two days before her passing at age ninety-six in January 2021.

Among Cicely's many roles was her 1978 portrayal of Harriet Tubman in *A Woman Called Moses*. Only a Grammy separated her from the Emmy, Grammy, Oscar, Tony (EGOT) pantheon. What contemporary actor would you cast in a movie about yourself, and why?

Gwendolyn Brooks

JUNE 7, 1917–DECEMBER 3, 2000

B orn in Topeka, Kansas, Gwendolyn Brooks was a child of the Great Migration, moving with her parents to the South Side of Chicago when she was just weeks old. From an early age, she possessed a keen observational lens into the souls of others, publishing her first four poems in the local newspaper at age eleven and receiving encouragement from Langston Hughes, to whom she had sent samples of her work. Six years and nearly eighty poems later, she became a regular contributor to the *Chicago Defender*, the local Black newspaper.

Championed by the great Richard Wright, Gwendolyn published her first book of poetry, *A Street in Bronzeville*, in 1945. Such portraiture of the African American community continued in her next collection, 1949's *Annie Allen*, the life story of a Black girl from childhood through motherhood told in verse. This work won her the 1950 Pulitzer Prize for poetry, making her the first Black American to receive a Pulitzer in any genre and only the eighth woman to receive the award for poetry since its inception.

In 1976, Gwendolyn became the first Black American woman inducted into the American Academy of Arts and Letters. While she welcomed this recognition, the growing impact of the civil rights movement led Gwendolyn

to re-examine the influence of her writing. She asserted Blackness as a political and social topic when attending a 1967 writers' conference at Nashville's Fisk University, and her oeuvre took on a sharper social commentary, evident in the 1968 long poem *In the Mecca*, about a mother searching for her lost daughter in a housing complex. The neighbors' disinterest in the mother's anxiety and the child's fate provided an arch and dispassionate commentary on a Black community on the brink.

In the 1970s, Gwendolyn parted ways with her publishing company, Harper & Brothers, and opted to align with smaller, Black-owned presses instead. She also began teaching youth—including teenage

gangs—to use poetry as a means of self-expression. In 1985, she became the first Black woman to be appointed Consultant in Poetry to the Library of Congress (a position known today as Poet Laureate). Whether serving in this role or teaching and mentoring in formal and informal settings, Gwendolyn Brooks was dedicated to edifying the lives of Black people—from the working-class urban communities to South Africa's Winnie Mandela—through poetry. Several of her mentees would become household names, such as Sonia Sanchez and Nikki Giovanni.

Write and decorate a poem in the style of Gwendolyn's iconic jazz poem "We Real Cool" (look it up if you're not familiar with it!).

Wilma Mankiller

NOVEMBER 18, 1945–APRIL 6, 2010

T he Indian Removal Act of 1830 initiated the forced migration of one hundred thousand Native Americans that came to be known as the Trail of Tears. The Cherokee were driven from their ancestral lands in Georgia and the Carolinas to the dry Oklahoma plains. Wilma Mankiller's family settled on a 160-acre plot, where the future first woman chief of the Cherokee Nation lived the first eleven years of her life.

Under a Bureau of Indian Affairs initiative to relocate Native Americans to urban centers, the family migrated again, this time to San Francisco in 1956. In California, Wilma's father became active in the labor movement. Exposure to progressive politics led twenty-four-year-old Wilma to participate in the Alcatraz occupation, a nineteen-month-long protest that began in 1969. Activists took over Alcatraz Island, the site of an abandoned prison, to demand self-determination, land rights, and restitution for centuries of systemic violence, brutality, and erasure "in the name of Indians of all tribes."

Wilma's passion for helping her Cherokee people continued throughout her life. Divorced from her first husband, Wilma returned to Oklahoma with her two daughters in the 1970s and worked to advance programs for rural housing, education, and health care. Despite a devastating automobile accident in 1979 that required her to undergo seventeen operations and years of painful rehabilitation, she kept working for change in the community.

"If I am to be remembered, I want it to be because I am fortunate enough to have become my tribe's first female chief. But I also want to be remembered for emphasizing the fact that we have Indigenous solutions to our problems." —W.M.

Wilma's leadership skills impressed the principal chief of the Cherokee Nation, who tagged her to run as his deputy chief in 1983. Two years later, she was elevated to principal chief, a role she held until 1995. As the leader of what was then the largest American Indian nation, Wilma saw Cherokee tribal membership enrollment more than double, going from about 68,000 to 170,000 members, and the Cherokee Nation budget expand to $150 million.

In addition to managing these material gains, she oversaw the development of rural health facilities and new resources to tackle drug abuse, as well as the expansion of the Head Start program, a US government initiative to provide early childhood and parent education, health, and nutrition services to underserved families. Wilma Mankiller was also a leader in the national feminist movement and a celebrated writer.

If you were the leader of a large community, who would you appoint to your advisory council? Why?

Septima Poinsette Clark

MAY 3, 1898–DECEMBER 15, 1987

Marches, speeches, and sit-ins are the bold strokes of social change, but it is the quiet, pragmatic work that alters lives. Such is the legacy of Septima Poinsette Clark.

Later referred to as the "grandmother of civil rights" by many, Septima was born at the turn of the twentieth century, when the discriminatory social, political, electoral, and economic effects of slavery were still very much present in South Carolina. As a student and later a teacher, Septima (who did not receive her BA until she was forty-four years old) experienced the catch-22 of Jim Crow. Education for Black people was inferior, when it existed at all, and she was acutely aware of the link between education and equal rights—crucial knowledge during the Jim Crow era, when voter suppression tactics, such as literacy tests or answering impossible questions like "How high is up?", were used at random to disenfranchise Black people.

Back in 1919, African Americans still weren't allowed to teach at public schools, so Septima joined the then ten-year-old NAACP to fight back. Working with future Supreme Court justice Thurgood Marshall, she mobilized students to get tens of thousands of signatures on a petition to change this law.

By the mid-1940s, Septima was juggling marriage, graduate

studies, teaching high school, caring for her ailing mother—and civil disobedience. South Carolina politicians, increasingly afraid of the NAACP, passed a law requiring all civil servants to quit the group. For refusing to do so, Septima lost her job in the Charleston public school system, along with her retirement pension, which she would not recover until 1976.

Undeterred, she moved to Tennessee and dedicated herself to teaching literacy and life skills to sharecroppers and other adults, showing them how to read, fill out forms, sign checks, and apply for driver's licenses. These grassroots workshops, which eventually became known as Citizenship Schools, spread across the South (one of her students was an activist named Rosa Parks) and were a precursor to the Student Nonviolent Coordinating Committee's Freedom Schools. Septima's advocacy helped seven hundred thousand African Americans become registered voters in the South.

"Literacy means liberation." —S.P.C.

Among her many posthumous tributes is 6238 Septimaclark, a minor planet that shines in the far-off heavens, a perfect homage for a woman who blazed a trail for many others.

Is there a new life skill you'd like to learn? See if you can find an online tutorial that teaches you how to do it. What did you choose, and why? How did it go?

Mary Evans Wilson

1866–MARCH 28, 1928

Were she alive a century later, Mary Evans Wilson—a civil rights activist, pioneering lifestyle writer, anti-lynching activist and orator, civic leader, mother of six, and member of Boston's Black elite—might have been called a Renaissance woman of her time.

Mary followed the typical educated woman's trajectory of schoolteacher before establishing herself as a health and beauty columnist for Josephine St. Pierre Ruffin's (see page 106) groundbreaking *Woman's Era* publication. In 1894, Mary married prominent lawyer Butler Roland Wilson, and the pair settled down in the tony Black neighborhood of Roxbury in Boston. But the racial and societal deficits during turn-of-the-century America directed Mary's attention beyond the pleasantries of tea parties and layettes. In word and deed, she focused her advocacy on discrimination in employment and medical care; segregation in housing and education; and the terrorizing rise of lynching.

Mary took to the podium in 1899 to deliver a keynote address to some three hundred concerned citizens at an anti-lynching demonstration in Boston's Chickering Hall. How could America drive Spain out of Cuba and the Philippines in the name of freedom while allowing Black Americans to be hunted down and murdered in their homeland, she asked—directly calling out the lack of action by the William McKinley administration.

Later, as more African Americans began to coalesce around civic advocacy in 1911, she helped her husband recruit thousands to Boston's local NAACP, the organization's first chartered branch. She even traveled across western New York, Pennsylvania, and Ohio to grow NAACP membership.

Mary Evans Wilson's enduring legacy, however, is as a cofounder of a group devoted to knitting warm woolens for soldiers (the eventual

Women's Service Club of Boston), which provided humanitarian aid in the face of continuing prejudice and inequality. Today, the organization offers hot meals, clothing and medicine, summer camps, drop-in educational resources, eldercare, and housing support for adults and children across Boston's social spectrum.

How can you incorporate activism or storytelling into your hobbies? Research the history of women's dissidence and protests for ideas.

Dorothy Toy

MAY 28, 1917–JULY 10, 2019

As a little girl, Shigeko Takahashi loved to do ballet and tap routines outside her parents' Los Angeles family restaurant. She adopted the name Dorothy as a result of her Catholic school upbringing. Under the tutelage of her Russian ballet teacher, she studied a muscular style of dance that involved Cossack kicks, leaps, and dancing on pointe—sometimes in the same four counts!

Even at the height of the Great Depression, Dorothy, her sister, Helen, and their friend Paul Wing had their sights set on fame. After appearing in a 1934 musical comedy called *Happiness Ahead*, they formed a dance troupe known as the Three Majongs. When Dorothy finished high school, the trio packed up a Model T and headed east to Chicago. Ultimately, Helen dropped out of the group to pursue a singing career, and Toy and Wing, as the duo came to be known, made their way to New York, the land of vaudeville and Broadway. Set to big band music, the duo's combination of soft-shoe tap, Lindy Hop, splits, and Dorothy's Cossack-inflected ballet made them an international sensation; in 1939, they became the first Asian American entertainers to perform at London's Palladium theater.

Toy and Wing wed in 1940, not for romance but to save on hotel stays. But with the advent of World War II, their fortunes reversed. First, Paul was drafted into the army, and then Dorothy's Japanese American parents were sent to an internment camp. While she was living in New York, a rival dancer outed her Japanese origins, sabotaging her career. When Paul returned from the war, he was a changed man, traumatized by the horrors of combat. And after the war, entertainment styles were shifting. Hollywood and Broadway no longer beckoned Toy and Wing.

Eventually, the pair divorced, and though Dorothy remarried and had children, showbiz never left her heart. Conforming to the changing tastes of the time, she mounted a troupe called the Oriental Playgirl Revue, which toured across the US and internationally in the 1960s and '70s. She also opened a dance academy in Oakland, California, instilling the joy of dance in generations of young people well into her nineties. Spirited until the end, Dorothy Toy died at age 102.

In the documentary *Dancing through Life: The Dorothy Toy Story*, Dorothy said, "When you're dancing, it's like you're in another world." What music inspires you to dance, transporting you to another world? Create a playlist that you can listen to whenever you need a pick-me-up.

Bridget "Biddy" Mason

AUGUST 15, 1818–JANUARY 15, 1891

B orn into enslavement, Bridget "Biddy" Mason was separated from her mother at an early age: sold, resold, and eventually acquired by Mississippian Robert Smith as a wedding gift for his new bride. The young enslaved woman's knowledge of agriculture, livestock care, midwifery, and herbalism made her a valuable asset on his plantation.

The Smiths, who had converted to the Church of Jesus Christ of Latter-day Saints, were part of an 1847 Mormon exodus to Utah. As a slave, Biddy was forced to walk the 1,700 miles on foot, enduring heat, cold, floods, and muddy terrain while caring for herself as well as the oxen and wares of the three-hundred-wagon caravan.

Slavery was discouraged in the Utah Territory, but Biddy and her children remained in bondage nonetheless. In 1851, Smith decided to relocate to California, a state where slavery was illegal. Biddy and her family had to set out on foot again, walking the four hundred miles to San Bernardino. At first, Robert declined to let Biddy and his other "property" know that slavery was illegal in California, but by 1855, he became concerned that his chattel would find out and leave him or that his neighbors would shun him, so he launched a plan to smuggle Biddy and her family into Texas and resell them. Fortunately, some of Biddy's friends who were not enslaved learned of the plot; they alerted the authorities, who eventually intercepted Robert's illicit caravan. After a court trial, LA district Judge Benjamin Hayes ruled that Biddy and thirteen members of her extended family were free on January 21, 1856.

> "If you hold your hand closed, nothing good can come in. The open hand is blessed, for it gives in abundance, even as it receives."
>
> —B.M.

Finally at liberty in Los Angeles, Biddy adopted the surname Mason in tribute to the Mormon mayor of San Bernardino, since enslaved people were not legally entitled to last names. She began to put her healing skills in nursing and midwifery to use. She saved money and bought land, and eventually helped to establish the First African Methodist Episcopal Church—the oldest African American–founded church in Los Angeles, and one of the city's largest to this day.

Biddy Mason also became a philanthropist, caring for incarcerated people, destitute children, and others. Amassing a treasure chest of $300,000 (what would be $6 million today) by the time of her death, she was considered the "richest colored [*sic*] woman west of the Mississippi."

The remarkable Auntie Mason is memorialized
in Los Angeles' Biddy Mason Park.
In your opinion, who deserves an honorary park?
How would you design it? Draw a sketch of it.

Bernadita Camacho-Dungca

MAY 31, 1940–FEBRUARY 15, 2016

....

I t's not every day that someone saves a language and revitalizes a culture, but many feel that Bernadita Camacho-Dungca did just that.

By the 1970s, the territory of Guam, located in the northern part of the Mariana Islands in the Micronesia archipelago, was losing its native roots. The Indigenous Chamorro people, who have lived there for more than four thousand years, had endured three centuries of Spanish conquest and three years of Japanese occupation during World War II. The dominance of American culture, food, and consumerism also made a significant contribution to the degradation of Guamanian identity. Guam is a distant US outpost central to the country's geopolitical interests, but the island's people are scantily represented in American government: Guamanian residents have partial US citizenship but are prohibited from voting in presidential elections and have only a nonvoting representative in Congress.

This was the national context that Bernadita, a linguistics scholar, observed when she returned to her homeland in 1973 to begin a teaching position at the University of Guam's School of Education. The plummeting

---

Ginen I mas Takhelo' gi Hinasso-ku
I Mas Takhalom gi Kurason-hu yan
I Mas Figo' na Nina'siña-hu, hu
Ufresen Maisa yu' para bai hu
    Prutehi yan Difende I Hinengge,
I Kottura, I Lengguåhi, I Aire I
    Hanom yan
I Tano' Chamorro ni' Irensiå-ku
    Direchu Ginen
as Yu'os Tåta. Este hu Afitma gi
    hilo' I
Bipblia yan I Banderå-hu, I Banderan
GUÅHAN.

—Inifresi, the Chamorro Pledge
of Allegiance

---

health, economic stability, and well-being of the Chamorro people were disconcerting enough, but before taking the teaching job, Benit, as she was called, had become increasingly aware of just how starkly language could be a portal to history and heritage. Interested in preserving the Chamorro language, Bernadita helped create the book *Chamorro Reference Grammar* and coauthored the *Chamorro-English Dictionary*.

Using linguistics to reclaim identity, tradition, and history, Bernadita worked tirelessly to bring up a new generation of educators who could teach the language and culture of the Guamanian people. Against the global dominance of the English language, which was becoming the lingua franca of the Pacific region, Bernadita's scholarly advocacy for Chamorro, as well as her efforts to promote local culture— contemporaneous with Indigenous rights movements in Hawai'i and among other Pacific Islander people— strove to help younger Guamanians regain pride in their traditional language and legacy.

Bernadita Camacho-Dungca is most remembered for having written the Inifresi (the Chamorro National Pledge of Allegiance) in 1991. Today, all Guamanian students from first grade up are expected to know this pledge by heart, and it is customarily recited by adults at all official public ceremonies.

What phrase makes you feel seen and proud of yourself? Practice saying it aloud in front of a mirror once a day for a week or two.

Florence Ebersole Finch

OCTOBER 11, 1915–DECEMBER 8, 2016

....

Because she had a white American father, Florence Ebersole Finch passed as a white woman even though her mother was Filipina. The privilege that accompanied her physical appearance allowed her to land a key strategic assignment as an underground agent in the Philippine resistance in Manila during World War II. At the Japanese-controlled Philippine Liquid Fuel Distributing Union, her job was to write out the vouchers for gasoline, diesel, and other fuel. Florence had a personal grudge against the invading Japanese, as her American husband had been killed on the battlefield in the war. Eager to help the Allied forces, she secretly redirected fuel, food, medicine, and supplies to American prisoners of war and freedom fighters.

Japanese authorities captured Florence in October 1944 and sent her to a prison camp near Manila, where she was confined to a two-by-four-foot space, underfed, and repeatedly shocked with electric probes. Still, she never revealed the identities of her fellow resisters. When American forces liberated the prison camp in 1945, she weighed a mere eighty pounds.

Once freed, Florence left the Philippines for her father's hometown of Buffalo, New York, yet she was determined to continue the fight and enlisted in the Coast Guard Women's Reserve. Finally, World War II ended, and she relocated to Ithaca, New York, with her second husband, hoping to

> "I feel very humble because my activities in the war effort were trivial compared with those of the people who gave their lives for their country." —F.E.F.

spend the rest of her days in obscurity and peace.

The US government did not intend for this hero to go unrecognized, however. In 1946, she became the first woman to be awarded the Asiatic–Pacific Campaign Medal. The following year, she received the Presidential Medal of Freedom—the highest honor an American civilian can earn.

A decade later, the US Coast Guard named its new Honolulu headquarters after her. Despite all her accolades, Florence Ebersole Finch kept a humble and low profile; when she passed away at the age of 101, her neighbors were amazed to learn about her illustrious history.

Who are some of the celebrated she-roes of your city or town? Reach out to them and see if you can get involved with their work.

Sojourner Truth

CA. 1797–NOVEMBER 26, 1883

orn Isabella "Belle" Baumfree, Sojourner Truth was one of the most influential Americans of any race, of any gender, of any time. Before she became an antislavery warrior, women's rights advocate, and legendary speaker, Belle experienced a traumatic childhood. The first time she was sold, it was at the age of nine, for $100. She would be sold three more times before adulthood. As a young woman, she watched as her boyfriend was beaten to death for visiting with her (slaves with different owners were prohibited from mingling, lest they conceived children and complicated ownership claims). She also became pregnant after a sexual assault and bore a child.

As her home state of New York crawled toward abolition, Belle's pitiless owner promised her liberation but reneged several times before another family "purchased" her for twenty dollars in 1826 and set her free when full Emancipation came the following year. That same family later helped her go to court in order to recover one of her sons who had been sold to another family; she won the suit and became the first Black American woman to win a court case against a white man.

In 1843, Belle underwent a religious conversion and took on the name Sojourner Truth. She moved to Massachusetts, where she joined forces with white abolitionists, suffragists, and proponents of religious freedom.

She met Frederick Douglass and others, began giving public speeches on the rights of women and the formerly enslaved, and dictated her memoir to a friend. *Narrative of Sojourner Truth, a Northern Slave,* published in 1850, cemented her renown, which sustained her as a public figure all the way into the 1870s speaking circuit. A foremother to Claudette Colvin (see page 40) and Rosa Parks, Sojourner rode the public streetcars in Washington, DC, in 1864, helping end segregation.

Sojourner also met with multiple presidents: Lincoln, to advocate for better working conditions for Black people, and Grant, to request he uphold his promise to provide land grants ("forty acres and a mule") to the formerly enslaved.

> "If the first woman God ever made was strong enough to turn the world upside down all alone, these women together ought to be able to turn it back, and get it right side up again! And now they is asking to do it, the men better let them." —S.T.

Despite Grant's inaction, she worked for his reelection and even tried, unsuccessfully, to vote for him. In her later years, Sojourner advocated for prison reform and the abolition of capital punishment. After her death, Sojourner Truth became the first African American woman whose statue sits in the Capitol building.

Because of her stature—nearly six feet tall and incredibly strong—and her non-European physical traits, detractors spread rumors that Sojourner was not actually female. While giving a speech in Indiana, she tore open her blouse in anger, exposing her breasts. Look up Sojourner's "Ain't I a Woman" speech, then write your own about an issue important to you.

Phillis Wheatley

CA. 1753–DECEMBER 5, 1784

Seized from her homeland in West Africa and subjected to the abominable Middle Passage aboard a ship called the *Phillis*, a young girl arrived at Boston Harbor in 1761. Because of her missing milk teeth, she was determined to be around eight years old. The harbor's slave merchant was thrilled that the Wheatley family was willing to take a chance on the frail child. From then on, the girl was known as Phillis Wheatley.

At a time when the Founding Fathers were penning the US Constitution and philosophers were opining that people of the African continent were subhuman, Phillis was mastering Greek and Latin and reading Virgil, Ovid, and Homer. By age twelve, she'd written her first poem, and at age fifteen she penned her most famous: "On Being Brought from Africa to America." In the latter, she pled for dignity for her people:

"In every human Breast, God has implanted a Principle, which we call Love of Freedom; it is impatient of Oppression, and pants for Deliverance." —P.W.

"Remember, *Christians*, *Negros*, black as *Cain*, / May be refin'd, and join th' angelic train."

Phillis wrote about contemporary issues such as the Boston Massacre and the Stamp Act, displaying an intellect that disproved the notion that Black people were inferior. The Wheatleys supported her as an artist, relieving her of some domestic duties, helping her master literacy, and even taking her to London in 1773 to meet other literary patrons. While in London, Phillis became the first African American to publish a book of poetry: *Poems on Various Subjects, Religious and Moral*. The Britons, who had begun dismantling slavery with a 1772 case called *Somerset v. Stewart*, encouraged the family to emancipate Phillis, but this didn't happen until after she returned to America.

The Revolutionary War and her marriage to an impoverished Freedman impeded Phillis Wheatley from publishing a second volume of poetry before she died due to complications of childbirth, but nevertheless, she is celebrated as a pioneering artistic voice during a time when women, both white and Black, were cloistered and silenced.

Although just 55 of her poems remain extant, it is believed that Phillis wrote more than 145 works. Write a poem about an important event in your life, then make a time capsule and place the poem inside for others to discover in the future.

Jovita Idár

SEPTEMBER 7, 1885–JUNE 15, 1946

While Jovita Idár was born into a relatively prosperous and well-educated Tejano (Mexico-US borderlands) family, she did not escape the xenophobic cruelties of what was called "Juan Crow." She believed in birthrights: education about one's history and heritage; suffrage; civil rights; economic prosperity; and greater choice for women around marriage and child-rearing. She used her voice and career in journalism to expand these rights on the US side of the border.

Writing under a pseudonym in her family's Spanish newspaper, *La Crónica*, Jovita criticized local politics as well as the poverty, English-only bias, and xenophobia that the Tejano community faced on a daily basis. One evening in 1914, rangers stormed the pressroom door of the family's second newspaper venture, *El Progreso*. Governor Oscar Branch Colquitt had dispatched the semivigilante law-keepers to punish the journalists for critical news coverage. Though small in stature, Jovita cited her First Amendment rights and shooed away the rangers, but they returned the next morning when the premises were empty and smashed the printing press to pieces.

> "Working women [recognize] your rights, proudly raise your chins and face the fight. The time of your degradation has passed." —J.I.

Despite intimidation from elected officials and community members because of her ethnicity and gender, Jovita remained engaged in human rights and justice issues. The brutal 1911 lynching of a teenage Mexican boy prompted her to establish the First Mexicanist Congress, a political convention that sought to address poverty, exploitation, and lynchings of

Mexicans and Mexican Americans. During the decade-long Mexican Revolution taking place just miles over the border, she volunteered with La Cruz Blanca Neutral (the Neutral White Cross), a medical relief entity founded by her friend Elena Arizmendi Mejía in response to the Red Cross's refusal to treat the insurgents.

Women's rights were also a top priority for Jovita. She was a cofounder of the feminist organization La Liga Femenil Mexicanista (the League of Mexican Women), which sought to advance education for Tejano students. In *Evolución*, the newspaper she founded in 1916, she often wrote about suffrage and the value of women.

By 1921, Jovita had moved to San Antonio, Texas, and turned her focus to naturalization rights and education, both as a journalist and through her involvement with the San Antonio Democratic Club. As Jovita Idár liked to say, "Educate a woman, and you educate a family." She spent the final decades of her life working as a volunteer English translator at the local hospital, starting a kindergarten, and raising her sister's children.

During the early decades of the twentieth century, discriminatory signs saying **NO DOGS, NO MEXICANS, NO NEGROES** were common in South Texas. Design your inclusive store window poster.

Mimi Jones

1947–JULY 26, 2020

The photo takes your breath away: A white man wearing sunglasses and a sport coat stands at the edge of a swimming pool, casually pouring a plastic jug of liquid into the water. Young activist Mimi Jones and another girl have terrified screams etched on their faces.

This is a portrait of racial hatred.

The scene took place during one of the bloodiest summers of the civil rights movement. Black demonstrators were valiantly putting their lives on the line to protest white supremacist acts of terror, from KKK bombs to police attack dogs. In St. Augustine, Florida, activists planned a "swim-in" at the Monson Motor Lodge to agitate against the whites-only swimming regulation and hotel policy, hoping that negative publicity about segregationist practices would sway public opinion and help move the stalled Civil Rights Act through the Senate.

"Courage for me is not the absence of fear, but what you do in the face of fear." —M.J.

On June 18, 1964, seventeen-year-old Mimi was among the group of seven protesters at the lodge. As the young people entered the pool to begin their swim-in, the motel owner, seeking to not only disband the protest but punish the youths, ran to a supply closet, where he found jugs of muriatic acid, a cleaning agent. He poured the chemicals into the pool; immediately the protesters felt the fumes burning their eyes. When the police arrived, they jumped into the pool—not to help Mimi and her fellow protesters but to arrest them.

The next day, photographs of the protest made the front pages of newspapers nationwide. President Lyndon B. Johnson, wary of the world's reaction to such abject American brutality, pressed senators to pass the bill, which they accomplished that very day. The hotel itself was demolished in 2003.

After graduating from high school, Mimi Jones moved to Boston and continued to support grassroots causes for the rest of her life. In response to the incident, she said, "It only strengthened my resolve and my lifelong commitment to challenge racism, inequality, and lack of justice for all."

Mimi became involved in activism as a teenager. What can you learn from someone younger than you? Ask them how they would like to change the world.

Mary Jane Patterson

SEPTEMBER 12, 1840–SEPTEMBER 24, 1894

Upon her graduation from Oberlin College in 1862, Mary Jane Patterson became the first African American woman to earn a bachelor's degree. She leveraged her education to become a groundbreaking educator herself, though many remain unaware of her influence on future generations.

In 1856, Mary Jane and her six younger siblings moved from North Carolina to Ohio, most likely as fugitive slaves. Establishing a new life in a region known for its vanguard abolitionists opened doors of opportunity. Mary Jane attended the yearlong Oberlin Academy preparatory program and subsequently matriculated into Oberlin College's four-year degree

track (a more rigorous, classics-oriented course of study, also called "the gentlemen's program") as opposed to the two-year track, which was generally geared toward women.

Unlike her classmate Edmonia Lewis (see page 178), Mary Jane had a great experience at Oberlin. Degree in hand, she initially took a schoolteacher job in Ohio before taking a role as assistant to her former teacher Fanny Jackson Coppin, who had become the principal at Philadelphia's Institute for Colored Youth. Mary Jane herself soon became a principal at the brand-new Preparatory High School for Negroes in Washington, DC. For a woman to serve in this role was already quite progressive, but she was also the first person of color to hold the position.

Never married, Mary Jane Patterson remained an active humanitarian in DC and dedicated her life to uplifting African American people. She joined nineteenth-century Black scholars and activists, such as Charlotte Forten Grimké (see page 190) and Mary Church Terrell (see page 172), in establishing the Colored Women's League of Washington, DC, in 1892. This group provided working-class women with training in domestic and social skills. The league eventually morphed into the highly influential National Association of Colored Women, which exists to this very day as a service organization dedicated to uplifting Black women and their communities, supporting education, and promoting leadership.

There are many ways to effect change in your community (protesting, charitable giving, letter-writing, and more). In what ways do you want to make a difference in society, and which causes are most important to you at this moment?

Mitsuye Endo

MAY 10, 1920–APRIL 14, 2006

The bombing of Pearl Harbor on December 7, 1941, led to unprecedented displacement of Japanese Americans to internment camps. Almost overnight, some 120,000 Japanese Americans—considered enemies of the state because they were of Japanese descent, spoke Japanese, or were practicing Buddhists— were stripped of their livelihoods and their freedom.

In 1942, a lawyer named James Purcell sought to mount a legal case that would end internment of Japanese Americans. Mitsuye Endo was deemed the model plaintiff— like all Japanese American state employees, twenty-two-year-old Mitsuye had been fired from her job as a typist at the California Department of Motor Vehicles soon after the attack and was placed in internment.

"The fact that I wanted to prove that we of Japanese ancestry were not guilty of any crime and that we were loyal American citizens kept me from abandoning the suit."

—M.E.

She was also a Methodist, had never been to Japan, and even had a brother serving in the US Armed Forces.

Understanding the case requires going back to the 1215 British ratification of the *Magna Carta*, which established the law of habeas corpus. This ruling decreed that governments had to establish legal cause for detaining any individual. Based on Mitsuye's exemplary lifestyle and lack of connection to Japan, her lawyer disputed the legality of her imprisonment. In 1944, after three prior Supreme Court cases challenging Japanese American incarceration had failed, the US Supreme Court unanimously ruled in her favor in *Ex parte Mitsuye Endo*. "The government," SCOTUS determined, "cannot detain a citizen without charge when the government itself concedes she is loyal to the United States." Suspecting how the case was going to end, the Roosevelt administration issued an order allowing Japanese American citizens to return to the West Coast the day before the ruling, thereby ending internment.

After the war, Mitsuye Endo and her husband, Kenneth Tsutsumi, whom she'd met at a Utah relocation camp, moved to Chicago and raised three children. Her parents and two sisters also moved to Chicago, and they lived out their days enjoying one another's company as free American citizens.

Mitsuye Endo's daughter didn't learn about her mother's contribution to legal justice for decades. Conduct a few mini interviews with older members of your family or community to learn about how you fit into the world.

Elizabeth Wanamaker Peratrovich

JULY 4, 1911–DECEMBER 1, 1958

While some may consider Dr. Martin Luther King Jr.'s "I Have a Dream" speech to be the culminating moment of the civil rights movement and the catalyst for the Civil Rights Act of 1964, it was another oration, delivered by a Tlingit woman twenty years prior, that influenced the first antidiscrimination law in the United States—Alaska's Anti-Discrimination Act of 1945. The speech was delivered by Elizabeth Wanamaker Peratrovich, a housewife turned civil rights activist.

Alaska was not granted statehood until 1959, but in terms of racial and ethnic discrimination during the Jim Crow era, it was on par with the rest of the United States. Elizabeth, an Alaskan woman of the Lukaax̱.ádi clan of the Tlingit Nation, and her husband, a Tlingit of mixed Native Alaskan and Serbian descent, experienced everyday exclusion and racism in Juneau. Hotels and other establishments refused to serve Native Alaskans, and housing discrimination and school segregation hindered daily life, even though Native Alaskan men fought on the fields of World War II.

As leaders of the Indigenous rights organizations Alaska Native Brotherhood and Alaska Native Sisterhood, the Peratroviches wrote to the territorial governor asking for change. He agreed to advance a 1941 antidiscrimination bill, which unfortunately ended in a deadlock.

Over the next two years, the couple encouraged their fellow

> "I would not have expected that I, who am 'barely out of savagery,' would have to remind gentlemen with five thousand years of recorded civilization behind them of our Bill of Rights." —E.W.P.

Native Alaskans to run for seats in the legislature. By the time a renewed bill reached the Alaska Senate, there were two more Native Alaskans in the chamber. Even so, Juneau's territorial senator Allen Shattuck described them as "people . . . barely out of savagery, who want to associate with us whites, with five thousand years of recorded civilization behind us," to which Elizabeth gave an arch reply. Her impassioned depiction of patriotic and honorable people suffering discrimination in ways great and small reduced the opposition to what a local newspaper, the *Daily Alaska Empire*, described as a mere "defensive whisper."

The bill passed eleven to five, granting "full and equal enjoyment" of establishments to all Alaskans and banning race-based discriminatory signage. Since 1988, February 16 has been celebrated as Elizabeth Peratrovich Day in the forty-ninth state.

Because of the all-encompassing demands and travel across the vast Alaskan Territory that their civic leadership roles required, Elizabeth and her husband made the difficult decision to put their three children in the care of an orphanage one summer. What is the hardest choice you've had to make?

China Mary

1839–DECEMBER 6, 1906

I f you imagine a tumbleweed boomtown of the Old West, chances are your vision is modeled on Tombstone, Arizona. Well known as the location of the shoot-out at the O.K. Corral, the town was home to many larger-than-life characters. Perhaps one of its most famous residents was known as China Mary.

Mary was not her actual name—neither were monikers like Ah Chum and Sing Choy, which people often used to refer to her—and there are indeed several women named "China Mary" in the historical records. (Back in the late 1800s, Anglo settlers couldn't be bothered to learn the real names of the Chinese laborers in the region. The men were often all called John and the women, Mary.) The daughter of a "Gold Mountain man," as Chinese men hoping to strike it rich in California's Gold Rush were called, *this* Mary became a legend in the "town too tough to die." Her many roles included owner of a general store that sold both Chinese and American wares and proprietress of the Can Can Restaurant, the favorite haunt of legendary frontiersman and gunslinger Wyatt Earp and his gang. She also dabbled in less reputable pursuits like contracting day laborers and running a gambling circle, a brothel, and an opium den. An elaborately attired, no-nonsense matriarch, Mary was notorious among the denizens of the town.

In a famously rough-and-tumble community (Tombstone had just four churches and more than one hundred saloons), China Mary was both feared and beloved. One of about five hundred Chinese people living in the town during the time of the 1882 Chinese Exclusion Act, she took care of anyone in need, even paying medical bills for destitute neighbors.

When her time came to depart this earth, most of the town of Tombstone showed up to send Mary off in traditional style. The carriage began its long procession to Boothill Graveyard—a then customary way to confuse evil spirits as the dead traveled to their final place of rest.

Make yourself a delicious cocktail, mocktail, or other festive drink and raise a toast to independent and resourceful women like China Mary.

Maria Montoya Martinez

1887–JULY 20, 1980

Maria Montoya Martinez lived her entire life on the San Ildefonso Pueblo near Santa Fe, New Mexico. She is admired for her experimentations with traditional Pueblo pottery styles and techniques, which helped both preserve and create more awareness about the Tewa people and their rich culture.

The Tewa are descendants of the Ancestral Puebloan people. After the 1540 arrival of conquistador Coronado and subsequent reconquests by the Mexicans and Americans, the six northern New Mexico Pueblo tribes settled into agricultural lifestyles and were converted to Christianity.

Still, the Tewa preserved their traditional ways of life as well as they could. Despite the advent of the railway in the 1800s and the ensuing arrival of cheap, mass-produced cookware, Pueblo people still used handcrafted ceramic pots for food storage, cooking, and ritualistic purposes. Under the tutelage of her aunt, Maria learned pottery-making—a detailed and somewhat ceremonial process that involved harvesting the clay at a certain time of year, forming the pot, sanding away impurities, polishing, decorating, and finally firing.

After a 1908 archaeological dig unearthed remnants of unglazed pottery from prehistoric times, academic interest in revitalizing the craft grew. Maria, who produced

> "Out of the silences of meditation come purity and power which eventually become apparent in our art: The many spirits which enter about us, in us, are transformed within us, moving from an endless past not gone, not dead, but with a threshold that is the present. From this time sense, for this experience deep within, our forms are created."
>
> —M.M.M.

the thinnest and finest pottery on the pueblo, evolved the technique. With her husband's assistance, she produced matte black-on-black polished pottery vessels that became sought after as beautiful art objects, not just utilitarian wares.

Despite her star status in the art world, Maria remained focused on her community. Like the oil painters of the Renaissance, she came to understand that her name carried elevated commercial value, so she began to sign the pots she cocreated with her husband and family as well as the works of other fine Tewa potters. In Pueblo culture, community and family are more important than the individual, so the practice did not feel dishonest to her. This mindset distinguished Maria from many of the creators whose works were displayed alongside hers in museums such as the Smithsonian, the Metropolitan Museum of Art, the Denver Art Museum, and in the homes of collectors. First Lady Claudia "Lady Bird" Johnson purchased one of Maria Montoya Martinez's pots for the White House and President Obama kept it on the desk in the Oval Office for the duration of his presidency.

Do something with your hands over the next couple of days. It could be weeding your garden, folding origami, or just making a yummy sandwich! Devote your attention to the tactile experience of creating or refining something with your physical handicraft.

Mary Jones

DECEMBER 12, 1803–UNKNOWN

Prostitution has long been called the world's oldest profession—and Mary Jones was nothing if not entrepreneurial. In the 1830s in New York City, lads paying for pleasure were utterly beguiled by this elegant and accommodating woman. She was an undeniably skilled purveyor, running a brisk business pitching the woo in the alleys and parks of Lower Manhattan. In the afterglow of the rendezvous, however, her clients would discover they'd been pickpocketed. They avoided reporting the robberies to the police, embarrassed to have solicited a prostitute, especially one who was a Black woman.

But eventually thievery became Mary's undoing. A laborer whom she had entertained realized, upon returning home, that his full wallet had been replaced with an empty one. He located the owner of the empty wallet and reported the crime to the police. When an undercover officer who pretended to be a client arrested Mary, he learned that she was transgender.

Even in a city with a libertine reputation like New York, the 1836 trial was a tabloid sensation. "The Man-Monster" was mocked in the press, and in the courtroom, someone even ripped the wig off Mary's head, eliciting titters from the gallery and likely causing trauma for the defendant. When asked why she impersonated women, Mary was blunt: She worked as a domestic in several brothels, where the "girls of ill fame" paid her to dress up as a woman for their entertainment. They complimented her appearance, and Mary decided to make a career of it.

After serving a five-year larceny sentence at Sing Sing Correctional Facility, Mary returned to "the life." In the summer of 1845, she was arrested for engaging in sex acts with men. The local newspapers had a heyday describing the elaborate prosthetic she used to mimic a vagina.

Today, Mary Jones is appreciated as one of the earliest known

transgender women in New York history. The filmmaker Tourmaline was commissioned in 2019 to create a fantastical short film portraying Mary's life. Entitled *Salacia*, it is part of the permanent collection at the Museum of Modern Art in New York City.

Think about a time when you felt that you had to hide an important part of your true self. Why did this occur? How do you feel about it today?

Charlotte E. Ray

JANUARY 13, 1850–JANUARY 4, 1911

Looking into the life of Charlotte E. Ray reveals a startling reality about the insignificance historically ascribed to Black American women: The photograph that surfaces most commonly when searching her name is indisputably *not* of Charlotte. A simple validation of the years of her life confirms this: She died in 1911, yet the photo generally associated with her shows a woman sporting the hairdo and clothing of the 1920s or even '30s, decades after Charlotte's death. Given that she was the first Black woman lawyer in the US, it is disappointing that her story has been visually misconstrued and erased.

Born to a middle-class family in New York, Charlotte attended one of the few schools open to African American girls at the time. She progressed in her scholarly pursuits and was accepted to the prestigious teacher training program at Howard University. While this was considered a great achievement for a woman, especially a woman of color, Charlotte knew that Washington, DC, was beginning to accept women to the bar. With ambitions of becoming a lawyer, she applied for admission. It is said she registered for the entrance exam using her initials—C. E. Ray—to deter notice of her gender.

On April 23, 1872, she was admitted to the District of Columbia bar. In addition to being the first Black woman lawyer, she was only the third American woman to complete law school. She opened a commercial law practice in Washington, DC, advertising in the local papers that catered to the burgeoning Black elite. Her most well-known case, *Gadley v. Gadley*, involved a domestic dispute where she represented a woman petitioning for divorce from an abusive husband. Charlotte argued her case before the District of Columbia Supreme Court in 1875, making her the first woman to make a case in the capital's highest court.

Despite these distinctions, clients were scarce and, like Mrs. Gadley, generally of meager means and social station, which rendered them unable to sustain the cost of legal counsel. By 1879, Charlotte had abandoned her practice and returned to New York to become a teacher once again. In her later years, she devoted herself to the suffrage movement and joined the brand-new National Association of Colored Women in 1896. Charlotte E. Ray passed away at age sixty in Queens, New York.

Are there other lawyers or activists you admire who fight for the rights of women or underrepresented people? Write about what makes them special.

Sylvia Rivera

JULY 2, 1951–FEBRUARY 19, 2002

Sylvia Rivera, a Puerto Rican Venezuelan activist from New York City, was known to say, "The streets raised me." Assigned male at birth, she was first abandoned by her father and then orphaned as a toddler when her mother died by suicide. By fourth grade, she was wearing makeup to school. Her grandmother tried to beat the effeminate mannerisms out of her, so at age eleven, she ran away. Living on the streets as a child sex worker, she was taken in by the drag community and given a new name—Sylvia—and the family she had never had.

In the mid-1960s, Sylvia aligned with both the Black Panthers and the Young Lords, but it was the Stonewall riots in 1969 that changed everything. Happening upon the uprising by chance, the seventeen-year-old witnessed the bar patrons in full revolt against another nighttime raid by the cops. She gleefully joined the melee. Coins, bottle caps, and eventually a Molotov cocktail were thrown. It is said the gay rights movement was born that night.

After Stonewall, Sylvia shifted her activism to support "her people," joining leading rights groups such as the Gay Liberation Front and later the Gay Activists Alliance. She became a staunch advocate for trans people's rights to legal protection, economic justice, and social dignity, cofounding Street Transvestite Action Revolutionaries, an organization that provided food and shelter to transgender youth who had been cast out of or run away from their homes, with fellow activist Marsha P. Johnson (see page 62). The group exerted political pressure that helped enact nondiscrimination laws in both New York City and New York State.

Sylvia grew increasingly disgusted by some gay activists' motivation to assimilate into mainstream society and leave trans people on the fringes.

"I'm not missing a moment of this— it's the revolution!"

—S.R., on the day the Stonewall riots began

She abandoned activist causes for twenty years, only reemerging in the 1990s to advocate for gay marriage and rights for LGBTQIA+ people in the military. Years of hard living had ravaged her health, and she died from liver cancer at age fifty. The Sylvia Rivera Law Project, a legal aid organization serving low-income trans people of color, was founded in 2002, that same year.

At the 1973 Christopher Street Liberation Day March, Sylvia delivered her famous "Y'all Better Quiet Down" speech, in which she passionately scolded the mainstream, middle-class, and predominantly white gay people in the movement and the audience alike, because she considered them uninterested in— and even dismissive of—her experiences as a trans woman of color. Despite the audience's scoffs at Sylvia's speech, she reminded them that she'd been beaten, jailed, assaulted, and left homeless, challenging them to "think about it." How do you recognize and honor the lived experience of others?

Sue Ko Lee

MARCH 9, 1910–MAY 15, 1996

The National Dollar Store should have been an immigrant success story. Founded in 1901 by Joe Shoong, the son of Chinese immigrants, it became a successful discount chain with nearly fifty outlets across the country. But the garment factory workers the chain employed were paid only twenty-five cents an hour. This was below the thirty-three and a third cents required by law, but between xenophobia and the ravages of the Great Depression, exploitative factory labor was the only work most Chinese immigrants could find. In 1938, the International Ladies' Garment Workers' Union (ILGWU) solidified its organizing in San Francisco's Chinatown in pursuit of two objectives: to end sweatshop conditions in the factories and to force Chinese-run factories to stop undercutting union shops and poaching workers.

Sue Ko Lee, a Chinese American garment worker at the National Dollar Store, became part of the Chinese Ladies' Garment Workers' Union, a local chapter of the ILGWU, which went on strike for better wages on February 28, 1938. Their nearly four-month labor stoppage was, at the time, the longest strike in San Francisco history. The workers received many of their demands, such as fourteen-dollar weekly pay, a forty-hour workweek, overtime, and better health and sanitary conditions, among other gains.

A year after the settlement, on the exact day the factory owner's obligation expired, he shuttered the San Francisco store. But many of the laborers were able to find jobs that

> "In my opinion, the strike was the best thing that ever happened. It changed our lives. We overcame bigotry, didn't we?" —S.K.L.

had previously been closed to Asian workers in other factories. For this reason, the National Dollar Store strike is celebrated for helping desegregate San Francisco's garment industry. Sue Ko Lee went on to become a union secretary and a delegate to the ILGWU national convention.

If you were starting a business, what five workspace amenities and five employment benefits would you provide your employees, and why?

Ida B. Wells

JULY 16, 1862–MARCH 25, 1931

As the fragile progressivism of the post–Civil War Reconstruction period gave way to the racialized backlash of lynching and the Jim Crow era, journalists played an essential role in exposing America's grim realities. Ida B. Wells stands out as one of the most courageous.

Born into slavery in Mississippi, Ida grew up in poverty and privation. At a young age, she lost both parents and a sibling to yellow fever. She graduated from Rust College, a historically Black college that her own father had helped establish. Ida had a fire for justice, and she went on to utilize all the tools at her disposal to advance the rights of African Americans.

Sometimes she sought justice through jurisprudence, like when she sued a Memphis train company for discrimination in 1884. If, as in this instance, the courts of law ruled against her (though she won at the state level, the 1884 decision was overturned in federal court), Ida strove for victory in the court of public opinion, using journalism and speaking engagements as her weapons.

The 1892 lynching of Ida and Mary Church Terrell's (see page 172) friend, shop owner Thomas Moss, enraged them both and propelled them into anti-lynching activism. Ida also risked her safety to travel south to learn firsthand about the deprived conditions African Americans faced and report their plight to America and the world.

She inflamed newspaper readers across the country when she posited that white women were capable of attraction toward Black men. (The "impossibility" of cross-racial affection, coupled with white men's fear and othering of Black men were often cited as justification for discrimination and violence against African American men, including lynching.) She even visited the White House in 1898 to beseech President William McKinley to support the anti-lynching cause but was unsuccessful.

After marrying Ferdinand Barnett in 1895, Ida had four children and juggled family life with her

"Somebody must show that the Afro-American race is more sinned against than sinning, and it seems to have fallen upon me to do so."

—I.B.W.

work. This included cofounding the National Association of Colored Women in 1896 with Terrell and Harriet Tubman (see page 200) and helping to form the NAACP in 1909.

Even though many of her white sisters in the suffragist movement were reticent to embrace desegregation, Ida B. Wells remained active in women's issues throughout her life. She was awarded a posthumous Pulitzer Prize in 2020 for "outstanding and courageous reporting on the horrific and vicious violence against African Americans during the era of lynching."

Ida, whose journalism illustrated an immense compassion for people in need, was honored with a public sculpture in her hometown of Memphis, Tennessee, in 2021. Plant a seed in honor of Ida or another foremother in this book.

Rebecca Lee Crumpler

FEBRUARY 8, 1831–MARCH 9, 1895

Inspired by her aunt who raised her and who used traditional healing remedies, a young woman known as Rebecca Davis left her home in Pennsylvania to become a nurse's apprentice in Boston. She was so successful in her training that her instructors encouraged her to continue her studies at the New England Female Medical College, since nursing schools did not exist at the time. This was an audacious move for 1860—women, deemed "too delicate" for the medical profession, were criticized for "taking the place" of male candidates, and only 300 of the 54,543 physicians in the United States were women. African American women? Zero.

A year later, Rebecca lost her medical school scholarship—undeterred, she found another. Two years later, in 1863, her marriage to former slave Wyatt Lee ended when he died of tuberculosis. Despite these setbacks, she finished her studies, and with the "doctress" degree finally in hand, Rebecca moved to Virginia in 1864. There, she found employment with the newly formed Freedmen's Bureau, a branch of government created to help the displaced former enslaved population gain means to

independent livelihood. Working with families in transition helped Rebecca discover her life's passion: caring for women and children.

Rebecca remarried in 1865, to an escaped slave named Arthur Crumpler. She returned to Boston, where she opened a private practice and had a child. As in the South, however, Rebecca experienced discrimination; pharmacists resisted filling her prescriptions, hoping to discourage patients from seeing her. Instead of closing her practice, she redoubled her commitment to medicine, writing the 1883 tome *A Book of Medical Discourses*,

reputed to be the first medical book ever written by a Black woman physician. Dedicated to "mothers, nurses, and all who may desire to mitigate the afflictions of the human race," the book promoted health care for mothers and children, from how to wash a newborn and breastfeed, to the prevention of cholera and measles, to the dangers of administering brandy and gin as pain relief (common at the time).

Rebecca Lee Crumpler is remembered as a remarkable pioneer who helped pave the way for more Black Americans and women to find success in the medical field.

When Rebecca passed away in 1895, her burial place in Boston's Hyde Park was marked with just a stick. In 2020, a local group of historians and neighbors rallied to purchase an appropriate gravestone for the physician. Is there someone unfamous you admire and would like to memorialize? Who and why?

Thelma Garcia Buchholdt

AUGUST 1, 1934–NOVEMBER 5, 2007

Born in the northern Philippines in 1934, Thelma Garcia raced through primary and secondary school, graduating high school at age fifteen and setting off for Mount Saint Mary's University in Los Angeles two years later, in 1951. A young but accomplished scholar, she completed graduate studies in Nevada and soon thereafter married and had children.

Alaska had only attained statehood in 1959, so when Thelma moved to Anchorage with her family in 1965, she discovered a community in major flux. The forty-ninth state was struggling to balance the enticements of oil discovery and a lucrative trans-Alaska oil pipeline with a commitment to environmental protection, as well as an obligation to respect and preserve the rights and lifeways of its Indigenous people. Thelma became active in civic life around Anchorage, the Last Frontier's biggest city. She cofounded the Boys and Girls Club of Alaska, was a member of the League of Women Voters, and eventually became the Alaska coordinator for the 1972 George McGovern presidential campaign.

Thelma's 1974 election to the Alaska House of Representatives was the first of four consecutive appointments to the state legislature, making her Alaska's first Asian American legislator and the first

> "All in all, I think our people are growing in Alaska. Many of the old-timers are gone, but the children talk about how wonderful their parents and grandparents were, the traditions they left: of work, ethical principles, family unity."
>
> —T.G.B.

Filipina American legislator in the United States. Her priorities included mental health, domestic violence, infrastructure, and dividend payout regulations. She also made significant cultural contributions, cofounding the Filipino Heritage Council of Alaska and authoring the definitive history book, *Filipinos in Alaska: 1788–1958*. In 2009, two years after her passing, Thelma Garcia Buchholdt was inducted into the inaugural class of the Alaska Women's Hall of Fame.

Improving mental health services was one of Thelma's passions as a politician. Take five minutes today to check in with how you're feeling physically and emotionally and to focus on your breathing.

Zarina Hashmi

JULY 16, 1937–APRIL 25, 2020

....

Like Etel Adnan (see page 76), Zarina (who went by her first name only) was a woman whose notions of homeland, exile, language, memory, and identity were greatly influenced by the geopolitics of her time. As ethnic violence exploded during the 1947 partition of the Indian subcontinent, Zarina, a Muslim, fled to Karachi, Pakistan. The trauma of sudden exile, the sight of human carnage, and the anguish of losing "home" would never leave her.

At age twenty-one, Zarina wed diplomat Saad Hashmi in an arranged marriage. Her husband's postings took the couple on an around-the-world tour of duty that afforded Zarina new forms of artistic inspiration. First was Bangkok, where she discovered printmaking. By the early 1960s, she was part of the art community in New Delhi, capital of her now estranged homeland. They then went to Paris, where the famous art school Atelier 17 introduced Zarina to abstraction and modernism. In 1974, she took a yearlong solo sojourn to Japan to study woodblock techniques with master artist Toshi Yoshida. Her international travels would also take her to Bonn, Germany, and Los Angeles over the years.

Zarina moved to New York City in 1976 and unfortunately became widowed the following year. She began connecting with feminist art collectives and visual artists of Manhattan's booming downtown cultural scene. As her art grew more experimental, she reduced her palette to black and white and worked across various mediums, including sculpture,

collage, paper relief, prints, and poetry. She also incorporated family letters into her work. They were written in Urdu, her mother tongue and the language of her spirit and dreams.

Though there were lean years, Zarina achieved great success during her lifetime. She was one of four artists selected to represent India at the country's first pavilion at the Venice Biennale (ironic, given that partition had later turned her into a stranger in her home country), and her art was the subject of retrospective exhibits around the world. Her works now sit in the permanent collections of many art museums, including the San Francisco Museum of Modern Art and New York's Whitney Museum of American Art, Solomon R. Guggenheim Museum, and Metropolitan Museum

> "I have had people come to my show and start to cry. I always ask them why, and usually they say, 'That is our story also.' A lot of them were people who were exiles from their own country: Holocaust survivors, or people who had the desire to return home. I realize that if you tell your story and if someone can come and cry on your shoulder, I think that is sharing."
>
> —Z.H.

of Art. A master of depicting longing and alienation in her art, Zarina Hashmi lived everywhere, anywhere, and, in some ways, nowhere.

Zarina's artistic use of geometry and minimalist, structural purity is attributed to her early interest in architecture and mathematics. Observe the objects around you for the next day or two. How can you distill these complex forms into circles, squares, or other shapes? Sketch the way you see them differently.

Mary Church Terrell

SEPTEMBER 23, 1863–JULY 24, 1954

Mary Church was born in 1863, the year the Emancipation Proclamation went into effect. Her father was thought to be the South's first Black millionaire, and her mother was a successful hair salon entrepreneur. After graduating from Oberlin College—Mary was one of the first African American women to attend the institution and one of the few women admitted to the "gentlemen's" four-year degree program—she became a teacher at Ohio's Wilberforce University in 1885. Two years later, she moved to Washington, DC, to teach at the Preparatory High School for Colored Youth (later known as the M Street High School)—the nation's first public high school for African Americans.

After embarking on a two-year tour of Europe, Mary returned to her teaching job in DC. A year later, she married the school's language department chair, Robert H. Terrell.

In 1892, Mary's family friend in Memphis, Thomas Moss, was lynched for running a general store deemed too successful. He was also a friend of Ida B. Wells (see page 164), and his murder propelled both women's anti-lynching activism. That year, they cofounded the Colored Women's League (which later became the National Association of Colored Women), working alongside a veritable who's who of racial rights advocates: Charlotte Forten Grimké (see page 190), Mary Jane Patterson (see page 146), and Frederick Douglass. With Douglass,

> "I cannot help wondering what I might have become and might have done if I had lived in a country which had not circumscribed and handicapped me on account of my race but had allowed me to reach any heights I was able to obtain."
>
> —M.C.T.

Mary unsuccessfully appealed to President Benjamin Harrison to publicly condemn lynching.

Mary used the lectern, the pen, the halls of power, and the streets to advocate for change. Across the US and Europe, she spoke out in favor of women's rights and against lynching. In 1904, she published a courageous article, "Lynching from a Negro's Point of View," in a prominent academic journal, the *North American Review*. One of her most well-known works was her 1940 autobiography, *A Colored Woman in a White World*.

Mary Church Terrell remained a fighter all her life. In 1922, she participated in a silent march to pressure Congress to pass anti-lynching legislation, and took part in sit-ins and protests well into her eighties. She lived to see two major

civil rights victories: Washington, DC's desegregation of restaurants and stores in 1953, and the 1954 *Brown v. Board of Education* ruling to end segregation in public schools.

Mary was a prolific journalist, publishing under the pen name Euphemia Kirk in both Black and white press outlets. Read the opinion section of a newspaper or news website for the next two weeks. What new issues did you learn about that you'd like to support or share?

Pablita Velarde

SEPTEMBER 19, 1918–JANUARY 12, 2006

Born on the Santa Clara Pueblo in northern New Mexico, Pablita Velarde was given the Tewa name Tse Tsan (Golden Dawn) at her naming ceremony. Life on the Indigenous land was rife with poverty and illness: Pablita's eyesight was damaged by disease, and her mother died of tuberculosis before Pablita's fourth birthday. In 1932, at age fourteen, Pablita was one of the first girls to enroll in the art program at Santa Fe Indian School, where she learned from art teacher Dorothy Dunn. Pablita and her sisters spent summers on the pueblo, learning artisan traditions from their grandmother and listening to ancestral legends from their father, a storyteller. Such lore later influenced Pablita's creative life.

Eschewing the famous earthenware pottery of the region (see Maria Montoya Martinez, page 154), Pablita adopted painting as her art form. Under the instruction of Dunn, she perfected a trademark style that influenced entire generations of Southwest contemporary art. With pigments derived from rocks and minerals ground with a mortar and pestle, Pablita's paintings translated Pueblo iconography into visual depictions of the Pueblo

> ## "A woman was supposed to be . . . a housewife and a mother and a cook. Those were things I wasn't interested in." —P.V.

experience and culture, from scenes of daily life to ceremonies and origin stories. These "earth paintings" featured dark outlines and two-dimensional, flat, opaque colors—a departure from the previous styles of Southwest painting.

Pablita tested social conventions as well as artistic ones. Painting was considered a man's activity, yet in 1933, she was selected as a muralist for the Chicago World's Fair at age fifteen. She was also the first in her family to earn a high school diploma, continuing to paint despite her father's wish that she attend business school. Later, her husband came to view her painting as too time-consuming—perhaps a contributing factor in their eventual divorce in 1959.

Pablita Velarde enjoyed a fifty-year-long career, from selling her paintings for fifty cents under the portico at Santa Fe's Palace of the Governors as an art school grad in 1936 to becoming the first Native American woman recognized as a professional painter. She received many international awards and commissions, including one by President Lyndon B. Johnson and another to create what is now an iconic series of murals at Bandelier National Monument in New Mexico.

Pablita's daughter, Helen Hardin, also became a celebrated painter. Is there someone with whom you'd love to share a creative practice? Write and design your partnership's manifesto.

Amelia Boynton Robinson

AUGUST 18, 1911–AUGUST 26, 2015

As a nine-year-old, Amelia Boynton Robinson accompanied her mother across rural Georgia to distribute pro-suffragist leaflets by horse and buggy. Her uncle, Civil War hero Robert Smalls, one of the earliest African Americans elected to the US House of Representatives, instilled in her a sense of civil service. When Amelia entered college at Tuskegee University, she studied under famed botanist George Washington Carver. Black Excellence was ingrained in her from childhood.

After a postcollegiate role instructing rural women in homemaking and nutrition for the USDA, Amelia married Samuel William Boynton in 1936. The couple dedicated themselves to the daunting task of registering Black voters in Alabama. When Samuel died in 1963, Amelia chose to continue their work by running for office. She became the first African American Alabamian since the Reconstruction era to run for Congress, and the first woman to run in the Democratic Party in Alabama. Though her bid for the legislature was unsuccessful, her 10 percent ballot count was remarkable, given the widespread suppression of Black voters in the South in the early 1960s.

In 1964, Amelia became involved in Martin Luther King Jr.'s Southern Christian Leadership Conference (SCLC). There, she helped plan a march from Selma to Montgomery to spotlight the African American struggle for voting rights. The march took place on March 7, 1965—now known as Bloody Sunday and a terrible date in US history. Led by John Lewis and Reverend Hosea Williams, six hundred protesters, including Amelia, attempted to cross the Edmund Pettus Bridge. Tear gas and whips awaited them at the other end, and Amelia, who was near the front of the line, was brutally beaten. The horrendous photo of her lying unconscious on the ground as a white police officer stood over her with a billy club made the front page of dozens of American newspapers, igniting outrage and public support for civil rights. When President Johnson signed the Voting Rights Act of 1965, Amelia was a guest of honor at the ceremony.

She eventually remarried and moved to New York for a time, then returned to Alabama in 1972. For the reenactment of the march on the fiftieth anniversary of Bloody Sunday, 103-year-old Amelia Boynton Robinson crossed the bridge in a wheelchair accompanied by Congressman John Lewis and President Barack Obama, who held her hand. This time, they were met by a reverent crowd.

"I have been called rabble-rouser, agitator. But because of my fighting, I was able to hand to the entire country the right for people to vote." —A.B.R.

In the 1970s, Amelia became associated with right-wing political activist and fringe conspiracy theorist Lyndon LaRouche. Her appointment as vice chair of his think tank, the Schiller Institute, was decried by many African Americans, yet she believed in his vision of a new world order based on the power of human creativity. Research an activist or social change group you'd like to get involved in as a volunteer or in some other way.

Edmonia Lewis

1844–SEPTEMBER 17, 1907

Though some have disputed the more fanciful details from Edmonia Lewis's account of her heroic life, her story is still a marvelous one to consider. In her retelling, she went from being a nomadic Chippewa (Ojibwe) and African American orphan living in wigwams in Upstate New York to becoming the toast of Roman society.

Wildfire (Edmonia's Ojibwe name) was orphaned by age twelve and raised by relatives. She earned her keep selling cultural artifacts to tourists visiting nearby Niagara Falls. Meanwhile, her brother struck it rich in the California Gold Rush and agreed to sponsor her education at Oberlin College, the first coeducational higher-learning institution in the US to admit African American students and confer bachelor's degrees to women. Even so, Edmonia experienced abominable discrimination: She was mocked by her peers and eventually accused of stealing from and poisoning two white students. For this transgression, she was beaten by a vigilante mob and left for dead. When she returned the following year to try to finish her degree, Edmonia was freshly accused of theft and ended up leaving school, though records differ on whether she faced expulsion or quit in frustration.

Casting this nightmare behind her, Edmonia moved to Boston in 1864. She enjoyed steady patronage for her portraits, particularly among abolitionists, whose social actions she greatly admired. Civil War hero and eighteenth US president Ulysses S. Grant himself commissioned a portrait from her once he'd left office.

By that time, Edmonia had moved to Rome, Italy, where she became part

> "I was practically driven to Rome in order to obtain the opportunities for art culture, and to find a social atmosphere where I was not constantly reminded of my color. The land of liberty had not room for a colored sculptor." —E.L.

of a high-profile lesbian expat circle. She spent the height of her artistic career there, enjoying prosperity as the first internationally recognized sculptor of African American and Native American descent.

Edmonia's neoclassical sculptures celebrate Black and Native American people, such as *Forever Free* (1867), which depicts a Black man lifting his arms free from chains, and *Old Arrow Maker* (1866), which features Ojibwe and Dakota characters from *The Song of Hiawatha* by Henry Wadsworth Longfellow. Due to her rising reputation, Edmonia was commissioned to submit a piece for the 1876 Centennial Exhibition in Philadelphia. Her massive 3,015-pound marble sculpture titled *The Death of Cleopatra* was disarmingly realistic for some viewers but a sensational work nonetheless.

As the neoclassical style waned in popularity, Edmonia Lewis left Rome in 1901 and quietly lived out the rest of her years in London.

If you were creating a massive stone sculpture, who or what would be your subject? Sketch it, perhaps from several angles.

Jane Johnston Schoolcraft

JANUARY 31, 1800–MAY 22, 1842

Jane Johnston Schoolcraft (whose Ojibwe name was Bamewawagezhikaquay, or Woman of the Sound That Stars Make Rushing through the Sky) achieved many firsts. She was the first published American poet to write in a Native American language as well as the first recorded Native American woman writer and the first known Indigenous poet. The most-heralded woman poet of the nineteenth century, Emily Dickinson, was born a full thirty years after Jane was born.

As a child, Jane learned about Ojibwe traditions from her mother. Her Irish fur-trader father taught her how to read and write, and he exposed her to his extensive library of nearly one thousand books—unheard of on the Western frontier. Jane enjoyed a privileged life in the Michigan Territory and even traveled with her father to England and Ireland. In 1823, she married Henry Rowe Schoolcraft, an Anglo American explorer and ethnologist. Henry was fascinated by Native American cultures and published an 1826–27 chronicle called *The Literary Voyager* or *Muzzeniegun*, considered to be one of the earliest ethnological magazines in the US. The entirely handwritten volume included some of Jane's poetry (even though she was not credited) and transcriptions of traditional Ojibwe folktales.

Jane's lyrical writing provided insights into Ojibwe lives and traditions as well as contemporary accounts of the political trauma faced

To my Maternal Grand-father on hearing his descent from Chippewa ancestors misrepresented

Rest thou, noblest chief! in thy dark house of clay,
Thy deeds and thy name, / Thy child's child shall proclaim,
And make the dark forests resound with the lay;
Though thy spirit has fled, / to the hills of the dead,
Yet thy name shall be held in my heart's warmest core,
And cherish'd till valour and love be no more.

—Excerpt from "Invocation" by J.J.S.

by Indigenous people during this era of forced relocation. Illness and chronic pain following childbirth consumed her life, however, and she died at age forty-two.

It was not until the twentieth century and the advent of women's history and Native American studies that Jane received recognition for inspiring one of the most popular poems of the American canon: "The Song of Hiawatha." Unsurprisingly, the fame was initially enjoyed by a man—Henry Wadsworth Longfellow's 1855 epic poem about an Ojibwe warrior is an homage to the lyrical "shores of Gitchee Gumee" near Sault Ste. Marie, Michigan, where Jane lived.

Jane Johnston Schoolcraft was inducted into the Michigan Women's Hall of Fame in 2008.

Jane's much-admired poem "Invocation" uses an ABBA CCDD rhyme scheme. Write two verses of poetry about someone important in your life using this pattern.

Mary Richards

CA. 1846-UNKNOWN

M ary Jane Richards. Mary Jane Bowser. Mary Jane Henley. Mary Jones. Mary Jane Richards Denman. Richmonia Richards. Richmonia St. Pierre. Many names for one incredible spy.

Virginia abolitionist Elizabeth Van Lew could not legally emancipate her inherited slaves, but she had young Mary baptized in May 1846, sponsored her education up north, and dispatched her in 1855 to Liberia, the West African nation founded by formerly enslaved people from the US. Mary did not like it there and wished to return to Virginia. Because local law prohibited emancipated or formally educated Black people from reentering the state, Mary was arrested upon her return to Virginia. By paying the ten-dollar bail, Elizabeth perpetuated the lie that Mary was indeed her "property." In reality, Mary was to become her coconspirator.

When Lincoln won the presidential election in 1860, Richmond, Virginia, became the Confederate capital. Elizabeth and Mary roamed the streets and slapdash prisons in disguise, bringing

food, clothing, medicine, and water to Union prisoners. They smuggled coded messages through the supplies and even helped some captured Union soldiers escape the dreadful Libby Prison, a former tobacco warehouse turned penitentiary known for its

disease and deprivation. The Union commanders began to increasingly rely on Elizabeth and her circle of domestics; indeed, by 1864, Elizabeth and all her servants (including Mary) were under the employ of the US government as spies.

Along the way, Mary married another slave of the Van Lew household, Wilson Bowser. It was around this time that the common though apocryphal account of "Mary Bowser, spy in the Jefferson Davis household" seems to have taken shape. It's said that she took advantage of her intelligence and the invisibility of being enslaved to supply her abolitionist mistress with reliable news. "When I open my eyes in the morning, I say to the servant, 'What news, Mary?' and my caterer never fails," said Elizabeth.

After the Civil War ended, a September 1865 *New York Times* advertised a forthcoming event: a speech by a "colored woman" named Richmonia Richards, one of Mary's many pseudonyms. In the address, Mary described her time as a Union spy and her current work organizing schools for Freedmen. Later on, Mary rejected Elizabeth's offer to return to Richmond and live with her; the formerly enslaved woman liked her independent life in New York. After that exchange, like a true spy, Mary Richards—and all her pseudonyms— disappeared from the records.

While historians are unable to verify the number of times Mary was in the Jefferson Davis mansion, a Black woman rifling through offices and papers certainly might have been dismissed as a nameless, illiterate person doing servile work.
Has there been a time when your "invisibility"— for example, as a woman, as a person of color, or for any other reason—worked to your advantage?

Sylvia Mendez

JUNE 7, 1936–

Jim Crow was not just a Southern scourge; schools, housing, and facilities in the western US were also segregated—separate but definitely not equal. In Sylvia Mendez's Southern California town, there were two elementary schools: the whites-only school, nestled among a bucolic row of palm trees, and the Hispanic school, a two-room wooden shack. Sylvia's aunt, Sally Vidaurri, had a French surname and light-skinned children, so when she went to enroll all the children at the whites-only school, she was told *her* children would be admitted—but not dark-skinned, Spanish-surnamed Sylvia and her brother.

The Mendezes were a hardworking family striving for a better life. Sylvia's parents were renting a farm from a Japanese American family that had been exiled to an internment camp—a poignant example of how complex and interwoven the immigrant-as-Other story has been in America. The Mendezes were frustrated by the racism they experienced. Even leisure activities were segregated: The municipal pool in Orange, California, was open to Hispanic children only on "Mexican Mondays"; the pool was then drained and cleaned so that white children could enjoy it the rest of the week, unsullied by waters in which Brown bodies had swum and frolicked.

In response, the Mendezes—later joined by five other Hispanic families and helped by Anglo activists—filed a lawsuit against four Orange County school districts on behalf of about five thousand Mexican American children, stating that the inferior facilities,

> "My mother always told me we are children of God and we deserve to be treated equally. Yes, we still have racism and prejudice, but we must persevere." —S.M.

resources, and educational access were discriminatory and relegated non-white students to pathways of menial labor and second-class citizenship.

The defense tried to suggest that the children had limited language skills or learning abilities, but Judge Paul J. McCormick, citing census law that categorized Mexicans as part of the "Caucasian" race, ruled that segregation due to national origin violated the Fourteenth Amendment. After several appeals, the ruling was upheld in 1946, eight years before *Brown v. Board of Education*. Governor Earl Warren (the future fourteenth chief justice of the US Supreme Court and a major catalyst for liberal progressive jurisprudence) moved to desegregate all public schools and other public spaces in California.

Eventually, Sylvia Mendez finished her studies and became a pediatric nurse. She has spent her retirement years speaking out against discrimination. In 2011, President Obama awarded her the nation's highest civilian honor, the Presidential Medal of Freedom, to recognize her role in helping end segregation in public education.

Mendez v. Westminster helped pave the way for the end of segregation against Asian and Native American students as well. What judicial ruling or law would you like to see passed in your name?

Mary Paik Lee

AUGUST 17, 1900–1995

Given that most Korean immigration to America occurred in the 1970s and '80s after the Immigration and Nationality Act of 1965, Mary Paik Lee's 1990 memoir, *Quiet Odyssey: A Pioneer Korean Woman in America*, is a remarkable and rare account of the early twentieth-century Korean American experience.

After Japan's victory in the Russo-Japanese War in 1905, Korea became a protectorate of Japan, and the homes of Christian converts, such as Mary's family's, were seized. The family fled for Hawai'i at a time when immigration of entire Korean families was rare. Mary, born Paik Kuang Sun, was one of only about seven thousand Korean people who immigrated to Hawai'i between 1903 and 1905.

After a year in Hawai'i, Mary's family moved to California. In her book, Mary writes that there were not more than three dozen Korean-born children living on the West Coast in the 1900s. Like most Asians, they faced harsh discrimination. In that era of American history, few bothered to make the distinction between Koreans and other Asian immigrants overtly targeted by the 1882 Chinese Exclusion Act. Therefore, though Mary's father had been a minister in Korea, he became a farm laborer in America. Her mother had to work as a laundress and a cook.

Mary also describes an American experience similar to those of many early twentieth-century immigrants: She was teased for having a non-Western name; she struggled to feel

> "It is very gratifying to me to see the progress our family has made from poverty to where we are today. It is nothing spectacular, but a good firm foundation has been laid on which our future generations will find it easier to build their dreams."
>
> —M.P.L.

close to the Chinese and Mexican children with whom she was lumped as an "outsider"; she saw her parents' determination to make their shantytown shack feel like a home.

Despite these early challenges and the later political unrest and war in Korea, Mary writes of a peaceful and fulfilling life. She grew up, married, raised three sons, and enjoyed old age, creating oil paintings in her small San Francisco apartment. A modest housewife, Mary Paik Lee never partook in the activism of the Asian American rights movement, yet her writing provides a meaningful window into a Korean American woman's resilience during a tumultuous time for both her ancestral home and her adopted one.

Write the first paragraph of your memoir.

Althea Gibson

AUGUST 25, 1927–SEPTEMBER 28, 2003

Lawn tennis wasn't Althea Gibson's favorite sport as a child. She was more interested in paddle tennis, which is played with a solid wooden racket and similar to pickleball. Althea, who won the NYC girls' championship in this sport, excelled in other athletics as well— so much so that at age twelve, she dropped out of school (although she later returned to get her degree) to focus on the sport she loved best: boxing. Nevertheless, it was lawn tennis that eventually catapulted Althea to fame. After her 1939 paddle tennis victory, she was offered a junior membership to Harlem's Cosmopolitan Tennis Club. The rest is sports history.

Within just a few years, she was establishing dominance in the sport. She was also making fashion

statements: Like future legend Serena Williams, Althea eschewed the conventional tailored dress in favor of a shorts-and-collared-shirt combo. When she won her first tournament in 1942, her outfit, combined with her tall, athletic build, had many mistaking her for a man or mocking her decidedly masculine appearance.

In 1946, two medical doctors who were also huge tennis fans approached the nineteen-year-old at the American Tennis Association tournament final. She thought their offer—to help her, a Black player, integrate the all-white US Lawn Tennis Association—had to be a joke.

But she accepted the offer, and with the help of other supporters, such as four-time US Nationals winner Alice Marble, Althea made her US National Championships (now called the US Open) debut on August 25, 1950, at age twenty-three.

At that match, the Forest Hills crowd hurled racist slurs at Althea. Then a lightning bolt struck a sculpture atop the stadium, hurtling the stone eagle to the ground and halting play. To Althea and her fans, it felt like an omen portending the changing times. Indeed, the following year, Althea broke Wimbledon's color line.

She sealed her place in history in 1956, becoming the first African American tennis player to win the French Open, and in 1957, when she became Wimbledon's first African American Ladies' Singles champion. (Arthur Ashe was the first Black American man to win Wimbledon in 1975.) When Queen Elizabeth II gave her the trophy and shook her hand, it was a hugely symbolic moment for Black people on both sides of the pond. Althea was also the dual

> "I always wanted to be somebody. If I made it, it's half because I was game enough to take a lot of punishment along the way and half because there were a lot of people who cared enough to help me." —A.G.

Wimbledon–US Open winner in 1957 and 1958. In all, she won fifty-six titles—eleven Grand Slams and six doubles crowns, two of which she won with her Jewish British courtmate, Angela Buxton.

In 2019, a memorial statue was dedicated to Althea Gibson at the USTA Billie Jean King National Tennis Center (the current site of the US Open), a tribute that King advocated for over many years. Only the second honorary statue on the grounds, it can be found on the southeast side of Arthur Ashe Stadium—a meaningful detail that signifies the tennis stars' shared history and impact within the sport.

Is there a sport or activity that you've always wanted to try but haven't? What research or planning might you put in place to give it a shot?

Charlotte Forten Grimké

AUGUST 17, 1837–JULY 23, 1914

C harlotte Forten Grimké came from one of Philadelphia's wealthiest African American families, with a lineage extending back to the Revolutionary War. Her early diaries provide a unique lens into the life of an African American woman of the antebellum period.

The Civil War enabled novel social ideas such as the Port Royal Experiment, wherein Black residents of the Sea Islands around Charleston,

South Carolina, were allowed to farm the lands freely, as long as they produced cotton for the Union war effort. Charlotte was among the teachers recruited to help these new Freedmen and their children attain literacy. In 1864, her glorious prose describing her discovery of her Black kin and their resilience and promise was published in the *Atlantic Monthly*: "It is wonderful how a people who have been so long crushed to the earth, so imbruted as these have been, — and they are said to be among the most degraded negroes of the South, — can have so great a desire for knowledge, and such a capability for attaining it. One cannot believe that the haughty Anglo-Saxon race, after centuries of such an experience as these people have had, would be very much superior to them."

After the war, she and her husband, Reverend Francis Grimké, were active in Washington, DC's elite Black social circles. Alongside other prominent Black leaders, such as Anna Julia Cooper, Mary Jane Patterson (see page 146), and Mary Church Terrell (see page 172), Charlotte helped establish women's clubs, which gave women places to gather and plan ways to advance social and political change. She helped found the Colored Women's League in 1892 and the National Association of Colored Women in 1896.

Throughout her life, Charlotte also showed interest in intellectual pursuits, including arranging lectures by literati such as Ralph Waldo Emerson. Charlotte Forten Grimké laid the groundwork for a new generation of African American intellectual and social advancement.

> "Oh, how inexpressibly bitter and agonizing it is to feel oneself an outcast from the rest of mankind, as we are in this country! To me it is dreadful, dreadful. . . . Oh, that I could do much towards bettering our condition. I will do all, all the very little that lies in my power, while life and strength last!" —C.F.G.

Charlotte taught her young students about heroes in Black American history, such as Toussaint L'Ouverture, leader of the Haitian Revolution. Who is someone you'd like other people to know about? Create a lesson plan that would bring their story to life.

Tsuru Aoki

SEPTEMBER 9, 1892–OCTOBER 18, 1961

B elieved to be one of the first Asian actresses to headline a movie in American cinema, silent film star Tsuru Aoki was a showbiz gal from the start. She emigrated from Tokyo to San Francisco with her aunt, uncle, and a troupe of Japanese actors in 1899. Hard times befell the company, and the young performer was raised by a family friend in New York before finding her way to Los Angeles and signing with a studio.

After a minor role as a Native American character in a 1914 film called *The Death Mask/The Redskin Duel*, in which she costarred with up-and-coming Japanese actor Sessue Hayakawa, Tsuru became romantically involved with Sessue. He went on to become an American movie star heartthrob—and her husband of forty-seven years. They were a remarkable Hollywood power couple during a time of increasing stereotyping and discrimination against Asians in the US. As the world transitioned from the Victorian era to the age of the flapper, Tsuru bridged mores by embodying two contrasting roles: traditional Japanese wife and spunky, modern American woman.

While her husband's star continued to rise over the midcentury, Tsuru stepped back from the cinema to raise their three children. She did not return to movies until 1960, when she starred alongside her husband in the drama *Hell to Eternity*. Not only was it the last movie Tsuru Aoki made before passing away the following year, but it was also her first talkie.

Silent movie actors had to rely on facial expressions
and exaggerated gestures to convey meaning.
Try sharing an important message or a story with someone
using only your facial expressions and gestures.

Madam C. J. Walker

DECEMBER 23, 1867–MAY 25, 1919

Sarah Breedlove, later known as Madam C. J. Walker, was orphaned at age seven, married at fourteen, and widowed by age twenty. She labored in St. Louis for almost two decades as a washerwoman and hair product saleswoman. Her own hair loss led her to experiment with different remedies, and by 1905, she was living in Denver, Colorado, and studying basic chemistry. When she concocted her miracle formula, Sarah used her third husband's name (Charles Joseph Walker) to launch Madam C. J. Walker's Wonderful Hair Grower. With less than two dollars in her pocket, she grew an empire that made her the nation's first self-made Black woman millionaire and a household name for many Black women throughout the twentieth century.

Madam C. J. started out selling her products door to door and advertising them in the Black press. As the social and cultural biases of the time dictated a European standard of beauty, business boomed. The Walker System— including shampoo and ointments for scalp health, lotions for growth, and an iron comb for straightness—gave Black women the very desired "processed look," which made many of them deliriously happy. As the business grew, she added nationwide mail-

order distribution and franchise offshoots in Central America and

the Caribbean, and opened a swanky flagship Harlem salon that her daughter ran.

Madam C. J. believed she deserved a certain cachet—John D. Rockefeller lived just down the road from her Westchester, New York, mansion—but she also adhered to a doctrine of Christian charity. She was a regular philanthropic donor to the NAACP and several African American secondary schools and colleges—causes all the more meaningful to her since she had been denied access to a formal education as a child.

For all her social status, however, Madam C. J. lived in an era of limited rights for African Americans and women alike. In 1917, she was among a group of Harlem civic leaders hoping to persuade President Woodrow Wilson to advance equal rights for Black World War I veterans, as well as designate lynching a federal hate crime. Frustratingly, the president flat-out refused to meet with the group.

Madam C. J. also sparred with rights leader Booker T. Washington, who was ambivalent about her promotion of European beauty standards. Infamously, at a 1912 National Negro Business League conference, Washington gave three men entrepreneurs center stage speaking roles but resisted giving Madam C. J. a slot. She made her voice heard anyway: "Surely," she proclaimed from the audience, "you are not going to shut the door in my face. I feel that I am in a business that is a credit to the womanhood of our race." Indeed, she was: The next year, Washington made Madam C. J. Walker a headline speaker.

"I got my start by giving myself a start." —Madam C.J.W.

Pamper yourself with a spa experience that would make Madam C. J. Walker proud. Bring out the candles, lotions, bubble bath, DIY face mask— whatever makes you feel your best— to create an indulgent all-about-you moment!

Buffalo Calf Road Woman

1850–MAY 1879

....

Facing America's post–Civil War zeal to claim the lands now known as Montana and the Dakotas, the Lakota, Northern Cheyenne, Arapaho, and other tribes sought to defend their ancestral Northern Plains homeland. The tribes fought in many legendary battles, such as the Battle of the Little Bighorn, where an alliance of Lakota and Cheyenne soldiers vanquished Civil War Union Army hero George Armstrong Custer and his men in what was known as Custer's Last Stand. Yet it wasn't until 2005 that members of the Northern Cheyenne tribe revealed what they had held in silence for more than a hundred years: It was a warrior named Buffalo Calf Road Woman (also known as Buffalo Calf Trail Woman) who knocked Custer off his horse and delivered the fatal blow to his head with a club.

It wasn't the first time Buffalo Calf Road Woman exhibited such battlefield prowess: At the Battle of the Rosebud on June 17, 1876, her brother, Chief Comes in Sight, was knocked from his horse. She charged toward him on her horse, somehow impervious to gunshots all around, and rescued him. This act of heroism energized the Lakota and Cheyenne, who went on to win the battle, later dubbed "Where the Girl Saved Her Brother."

As the unfortunate history goes, the tribes won the battle but lost the war. After Little Bighorn, where all 210 of Custer's men were lost, the US Army seized the sacred Black Hills from the Lakota tribe, one of the final acts of US military decimation. Buffalo Calf Road Woman, her husband Black Coyote, and others were eventually captured and relocated to present-day Oklahoma. As they tried to rejoin their homelands in the Northern Cheyenne Exodus of 1878–79, the turmoil of warfare and exile broke Black Coyote's spirit: Increasingly erratic, he died in late 1890. Some accounts say he died by suicide, but it is generally believed he was hanged by the US forces. Buffalo Calf Road Woman died of diphtheria and was buried in an unmarked grave somewhere in Montana.

Although it took more than a century for her contributions to be recognized, Buffalo Calf Road Woman is now remembered as a symbol of women's strength and fearlessness.

"Calf Trail Woman had a six-shooter, with bullets and powder, and she fired many shots at the soldiers. She was the only woman there who had a gun."

—Antelope Woman (Kate Bighead), Cheyenne Indian

Visit native-land.ca to see a map of Indigenous homelands across the globe. Does this map change the way you think about your city, state, or country?

Dolores Huerta

APRIL 10, 1930–

Dolores Clara Fernández Huerta's earliest role model was her mother, Alicia Fernández. At the hotel she ran in the agricultural hub of Stockton, California, Alicia always made a place for African American, Chinese, Filipino, Japanese, and Mexican workers— free of charge, if need be. With a college degree in hand, Dolores married, became a mother herself, and began her career teaching farmworkers' children.

Having daily contact with so many children who came to school with empty stomachs and bare feet heightened her compassion for migrant and agricultural families, who were often deprived and mistreated. Farmworkers, including short-term migrants, new immigrants, and their American-born children, labored under deplorable conditions, earning less than a dollar an hour without rest periods or cold water to drink. Dolores became fired up over their plight and the constant threat of violence at the hands of bosses and xenophobic townspeople.

After founding a workers' rights association in Stockton, Dolores met a young activist named César E. Chávez through their shared

network. In 1962, they launched the National Farm Workers Association union, which later became the United Farm Workers of America (UFW), one of the most transformative labor organizations in US history. By 1975, UFW had improved conditions for farmworkers, securing their right to collective bargaining and expanding their access to services such as food stamps and health insurance.

Dolores was just as influential in the organization as Chávez, though for many years the man was given most of the credit. The two activists did not always see eye to eye, and they got into epic arguments. Dolores was never one to wither in front of a man, and she often prevailed in their disputes. This was during feminism's second wave, and Dolores became a central figure in the women's rights movement as well.

Though she has continually advocated for nonviolent action,

> **"We must use our lives to make the world a better place to live, not just to acquire things. That is what we are put on the earth for."** —D.H.

Dolores did not always receive the same treatment. She was beaten by a police officer while protesting George H. W. Bush's presidential candidacy in San Francisco; the public outcry was such that the city instituted new policies on crowd control and police discipline. The powerful Teamsters Union, whose members brutalized and threatened many farmworkers at the beginning of Dolores's career, are now allies in UFW's mission.

In 2003, the lifelong activist launched the Dolores Huerta Foundation, which advocates for migrants' and farmworkers' rights.

Dolores is known for coining the slogan of the farmworkers' movement: "¡Sí, se puede!" (Yes, we can!). What would your activist slogan be?

Harriet Tubman

BETWEEN 1820 AND 1822-MARCH 10, 1913

S py, scout, army nurse, traditional healer, legend: There are so many ways to describe Araminta Ross, known to the world as Harriet Tubman. As chief conductor of the Underground Railroad—a network of safe houses and hidden routes that enslaved people used to escape the South—for more than a decade, she helped lead some seventy escaped slaves northward to freedom. She never lost a passenger to recapture, injury, or death. Harriet instilled a sense of discipline and resolve in her passengers, knowing that if one turned back, the whole party would be threatened. Brandishing her gun, she told her charges, "You'll be free or die."

Harriet deplored the injustice of slavery all her life. At age twelve, she was hit in the head by a heavy iron while trying to stop the beating of an enslaved person who had tried to escape. This injury not only rendered her partially blind but also led to a lifetime of severe headaches, narcolepsy, and visions. These divine apparitions are what Harriet said helped her "know" which routes to take when traveling north.

Harriet's first escape was her own, in 1849. Showing tremendous bravery, she subsequently returned to the South at least a dozen more times to help family and community members escape. Her knowledge of the back roads and celestial mapping as well as her ability to disguise herself proved helpful at the outbreak of the Civil War. Dressed as an old woman, Harriet attracted

little attention and was able to gather important intelligence about the Confederate Army's location.

Harriet was the first woman to lead an armed military maneuver in the US; she was also a Union spy and scout and a nurse who used traditional root medicine to heal wounded soldiers. Once the war ended, she raised money to help Freedmen get on their feet and for women's suffrage. She lived her final years in Upstate New York, where she established the Harriet Tubman Home for the Aged in 1896 and cared for her adopted daughter.

"I was the conductor of the Underground Railroad for eight years, and I can say what most conductors can't say—I never ran my train off the track and I never lost a passenger." —H.T.

Harriet Tubman's husband refused to accompany her on her first escape, and she later discovered that he had remarried. But the best revenge is living well: After the Civil War, she wed a Union Army vet twenty years her junior. Write the lyrics to the "diss song" about her first husband. Here are some rhyming sets to get you started:

Survive–Alive–Thrive

Weak–Sleek

Strong–Wrong

Hurt–Shirt–Skirt

Moving on–Feeling strong

Fool–Cool

Tomorrow–Sorrow

Forgettable–Regrettable

Broken–Unspoken

Pain–Gain

Years–Fears–Tears

Heart–Smart–Part

Yuri Kochiyama

MAY 19, 1921–JUNE 1, 2014

A nisei (second-generation Japanese American) might seem an unlikely poster child for Black Power, but Yuri Kochiyama knew firsthand that liberation struggles are connected. Even toward the end of her life, Yuri fought discrimination against Arab and Muslim people, linking early twenty-first-century Islamophobia to the xenophobic trauma she experienced during World War II.

For the first two decades of her life, Yuri lived a charmed SoCal life: She was a member of the high school tennis team and student union vice president, and she received a journalism degree from Compton Community College. She was well-liked, studious, and ambitious. But the 1941 attack on Pearl Harbor changed everything. Like one hundred thousand other Japanese Americans, Yuri was ripped away from the world she knew and sent to an internment camp. Her father, who was recovering from surgery, was arrested, labeled a prisoner of war, and treated as an enemy combatant—a baseless charge. He died soon after his release from a federal penitentiary.

By the early 1960s, Yuri and her husband, Bill, were raising their six children in a public housing project in Harlem, where the family experienced systemic discrimination, including subpar education. In the aftermath of the 1963 Birmingham, Alabama, church bombing that killed four innocent girls, Yuri became an outspoken advocate for Asian American rights, third-world liberation, and more. Her home became a meeting hub

> "Life is not what you alone make it. Life is the input of everyone who touched your life and every experience that entered it. We are all part of one another." —Y.K.

for neighborhood empowerment committees such as the Harlem Community for Self-Defense, as well as the militant Puerto Rican self-determination group the Young Lords. Yuri was also a member of Asian Americans for Action, linking the Asian American rights movement to the Black liberation struggle.

At a labor protest in 1963, she met Malcolm X and thanked him for all he was doing for his people. Soon after, Yuri joined his racial justice group, the Organization of Afro-American Unity, and introduced him to atomic bomb survivors and peace activists. In an iconic *Life* magazine photo, it is she who cradles the head of her wounded friend on the day of his assassination.

With her husband at her side, Yuri Kochiyama kept the fight going for decades, successfully lobbying for the enactment of the 1988 Civil Liberties Act, which provided cash reparations to all living Japanese American internment camp survivors as well as a formal government apology. As soon as Ronald Reagan signed the law, she asked for similar restitution for African Americans, descendants of more than four hundred years of slavery.

When asked about her life's mission, Yuri said, "The legacy I would like to leave is that people try to build bridges and not walls." What would you like to be remembered for?

ACKNOWLEDGMENTS

I want to thank Rachael Mt. Pleasant and Jaha Alamgir for their patient, painstaking, and precise editing; a girl can get spoiled! I'd also like to thank the rest of the Workman crew—Becky Terhune, Barbara Peragine, Kim Daly, Anna Dobbin, Amanda Hong, Erica Jimenez, Claire Gross, Moira Kerrigan, and Kate Oksen. I'm so thrilled to have collaborated with my jeune soeur Joelle Avelino, a magnificently talented illustrator.

Personally, I am so grateful for my own Brave Sisses: my mother, Florence Floranz; my sisters, Denise Jones and Alison Floranz; my daughters, Jasmine and Jade Kennedy (future Brave Sisses or whatever Gen Z will call themselves). My "dope kaleidoscope" of many Black, Brown, white, Asian, Indigenous, young, old, gay, straight, beloved sister friends living all over the globe—you inspire the breadth of the Brave Sis lens and the wide-open-armed welcoming of white women and women from around the world into this sister circle.

Thank you to Betsy Gleick for introducing me to Workman Publishing and for editing *The Zephyr* with me at Brearley all those years ago. I never gave up on writing and am thrilled these stories have moved through me.

Thank you to my Original Brave Sis, my grandmother Alice Green, whose spirit looms large in every bridge I build to the past.

Of course, thank you to my encouraging, loving, supportive Brave Bro, John Kennedy.

Finally, thank you for coming with me—and us—on this wondrous trip into history and back.